THE EPISTLE TO THE
HEBREWS

The Epistle to the Hebrews

Its Sources and Message

By

V. BURCH, D.D.

"Call me not so often back,
Silent voices of the dead,
To the lowland ways behind me."

LONDON
WILLIAMS & NORGATE LTD.
GREAT RUSSELL STREET

First published in 1936

PRINTED IN GREAT BRITAIN

To

DANIEL LAMONT

MODERATOR OF THE CHURCH OF
SCOTLAND ; PROFESSOR OF PRAC-
TICAL THEOLOGY, NEW COLLEGE,
EDINBURGH

WHOSE MIND AND WORK
ARE AKIN WITH THE WRITER
TO THE HEBREWS

CONTENTS

CONTENTS

PREFACE

THIS book is based upon lectures given to my students when I was Cathedral Lecturer in Divinity at Liverpool. Our two principal conclusions, that the Epistle was throughout Hebrew in ideas ; and that it was meant to aid Hebrew Christians who, because of contemporary and radical crisis in Israel's history, found it hard not to yield to the spell of " the silent voices of the dead," have been confirmed by the discoveries which it now sets forth.

V.B.

CHAPTER I

THE way towards new material for the interpretation
of the Epistle is best taken on a road we already know.
Commentaries and studies on the delightful document
are very many. They offer us a metalled way. It is
a very long one. It stretches from the third to the
twentieth century. For most of its length, then, an
ancient and straight road. Thus it reminds one of the
most famous ways which strike across Britain. Paths
worn by the feet of our forefathers pass into the ordered
chariot-ways of the Romans, and these into our own
roadways upon which men and women flash with the
haste of to-day. The way is the same. Its width
differs. The manners of transport have changed.
You have only to dig beneath its surface and modern
British motorist passes into Roman charioteer, and he
in turn into primitive British pedestrian. There is
nothing more traditional than that road, except it be
a biblical commentary. That is why we must take the
way which has been named. Through it we will cut
a cross-section. Thus we shall be permitted to notice
how direction, material and uses were ordained from
the beginning. To see if what moves on its surface

is more efficient, scientific and swift ; and therefore vehicles of truth. And to conclude at least that they do not follow the ruts of the chariots because they are wider, nor the footprints of the first men because they do not allow us to walk. Still they go over the same roadway.

The most recent and learned commentary on the Epistle is that by Moffatt.[1] When studied with the care it demands, and as it ought to be in the light of its long line of predecessors, this conclusion cannot be escaped. It reads like the rounding off of a great stage of interpretation. Or if we keep to our metaphor, scholarship has done everything to ensure the surface of and devise transport upon the traditional road. The direction of Plato and Philo ; the material of Chrysostom[2] and Gregory of Nyssa[3] ; the uses of Bengel[4] and Westcott[5] are conserved. Conditions are a little broadened or more straightly aligned. The surface is smoother than ever before. The amenities which subserve our traffic upon it are greater in number.

Let then a cross-section be cut at the point of its progress which is marked by Moffatt's work. Layer upon layer is exposed as if we were looking at geological deposits. Patristic layers with Athenian and Alexandrian characteristics ; Reformation layers with these characteristics so treated as to be turned into theological doctrines ; layers of the late historic period where the Fathers and the theologians are moulded into philoso-

---

[1] *The Epistle to the Hebrews* (1924).
[2] Ed. Eton, 1613, iv, 427 ff.
[3] *Patr. Græca*, xlvi.
[4] *Gnomon Novi Testamenti ... sensum cælestium indicatur* (1742).
[5] *The Epistle to the Hebrews* (1890).

phical Christology. Upon these is Moffatt's deposit which on analysis shows the use of Athens and Alexandria in equal proportions. The blending of patristic and mediæval views produces a doctrine of the Christ of the Epistle which unites the Cappadocian ideas of Gregory, the Cambridge ideas of Westcott and the Edinburgh ideas of Davidson.[1] A Reformation theologian could walk here with unimpeded foot. Modern critical findings are toned into the whole of his material so that Chrysostom might exclaim : it is an easier road than mine but it is the same road. Its smooth efficiency inclines its users to conclude that this must be the right highway. It appears to raise no questions. It thrusts itself across the centuries, between the twentieth and the first, as if there could be no other way. There is apparently a Roman appearance about it, although so much that is Greek has gone to compose it. The road of the commentators may be firm and long. There is august sanction for asking whether it has been constructed by tradition or truth. If we stand away from it and view it as we should any other historic development, that question takes on its fitting form.

To hellenise or to hebraise, that is the question of questions for the interpretation of the Epistle to the Hebrews. This does not mean that the commentaries have swung with the motion of a pendulum, now to the hellenic and then to the hebraic pole. It is the Epistle itself which thrusts that question upon the commentators and ourselves. Not because it was written in Greek, nor because early opinion said it was

[1] *The Epistle to the Hebrews* (1899).

written by S. Paul. But because it desires to be heard in its own terms. We are learning that Greek written in Palestine is sometimes almost more hebraic than Hebrew. Also that a manuscript notice of authorship is sometimes no more than a guess or predilection on the part of a copyist. We are awakening as well to understand that New Testament documents can be informed, as delicate organisms are informed, by tinctures which colour them in a new way. We are finding too that unlike those delicate organisms the novel colour does not help us to see them better ; but that the documents come out to us in a guise other than their own, hellenic or hebraic, according to the colour we had used. Some textual critics are aware of these exquisite matters. Most commentators remain unaware of them. There is emerging then a potent reason why we should realise their importance both as illuminants and non-illuminants of the text of whatever book of the New Testament they comment upon. Either they have been giving us or hiding from us the sense of the book. Therefore, we ought to interrogate and not to surrender to them. Quite a number of students of commentaries will retort : we do this already, for none among us thinks that patristic commentators were specially inspired of God. It is supposed that there is modernity in that attitude. But a stiff back towards the Past is often accompanied by weakness in the knees towards the Present. The commentary of to-day, especially if it be the work of one who is an enthusiast for the comparative study of religions, has almost hypnotic influence over those who can treat the Past with scant respect. What we refuse to an ecclesiastical estimate of certain commentators, we must deny to a scientific estimate of other commentaries. What God did not, the goddess *Scientia* cannot do. It will be better, however, to classify these books rather than to put controversial values upon them.

We can classify them, if we please, as pre-scientific and scientific commentaries. Or if we are a little troubled by such a literary division, we may use a temporal one. The mark " ancient commentaries " can be put on some and the mark " modern commentaries " on others. This division has its difficulties. For wherever we place the dividing line between old and new, we shall find that neither way shows that its writers had such an eager grasp of the question of questions and, therefore, they will go hellenic or hebraic as those who are compelled to take sides. It is good that they do not. It is not good, however, to find them almost unconscious of the question and more than inclined to go hellenic all the time. But does this unanimity in convention mean that the truth of the Epistle has been discerned ? Or must not the lack of sensitiveness towards the question of questions point that there is still much to be learnt concerning it ? That is a dilemma which can be solved in part by studying the ways of the commentators with our document. Why do they hellenise the Epistle ?

The first suggestion of a natural division among the commentaries would seem to be the doctrinal and the philosophical ones. Those which descend from Chrysostom and those from Gregory of Nyssa. The Antiochian preacher certainly bases his *Homilies* upon

B

the notion of the Pauline authorship of the Epistle, and Gregory assimilates its thought with Athenian philosophy. That makes a clear pre-scientific division. Does it hold for what we call the scientific period ? Take the last fifty years of commentaries. Chrysostom is virtually childless after Biesenthal[1] who is at the beginning of this chosen period. The idea of Paul as the author of the Epistle was soon set aside. That robbed Chrysostom of sons by direct descent. There are those who are of his family by indirect descent. They declare for Pauline doctrine in the Epistle.[2] Heigl[3] is an example of those who hold this view, though this does not mean that the Apostle was the author of the Epistle. A number of its students, however, do not consider that its ideas are Pauline. Thus this first suggestion of natural classification breaks down. It is not simple enough.

The second suggestion is that we should designate the Epistle as being, first, Christological ; and second, as having Athenian or Alexandrian colour, Take this division back among the pre-scientific commentators and we find, for instance, that both Chrysostom, in lighter tones, and Gregory, in deeper tones, are Athenian in colour. Both of them merge smoothly into the Athenian colour of the greater Creeds.[4] They are now the heads of a notable line of descendants, especially among Anglicans. Westcott is a son. He

---

[1] *Das Trostschreiben des Apostels Paulus An die Hebräer* (1878).

[2] *E.g.*, Lebreton, *Les Origines du Dogme de la Trinité* (1910), i, 345.

[3] *Verfasser und Adresse des Briefs An die Hebräer* (1905).

[4] *E.g.*, Chrysostom, *Hom.*, ii, iv, 437 (Eton ed.), where the Antiochian deals with ἀπαύγασμα—ὡς φῶς ἐκ φωτός.

may declare that the Epistle is " characteristically Palestinian " ; but the Christology he educes from it is clad in the robes of the Academy and could not wear a gaberdine. Nairne[1] is another descendant, and is often more platonic than the earlier Cambridge Platonists. Inge[2] seems to make it an Anglican virtue to put the Epistle between the writings of Plato and Plotinus. In what degree these descendants show that their Athenianism is subordinate to the thought of the Epistle or the Epistle subordinate to Athenianism is a subject we need not here search into. Both sorts are represented among them. The little less or more in either does not alter the fact that Plato is their illustrious ancestor.

Whether we are to see a fresh growth of his family the near future will tell us. If it is to be, the enlargement will come through Aristotle. Theirs will be Platonism with a difference. The Roman Encyclical[3] which set Aquinas in a stronger position than had been his in his own century has already called out eulogies of his commentaries as well as allegiance to his philosophical works. The development of what he wrote about the Epistle may even yet depose Greek for Latin exegesis. It is easy to see how its ideas can be given a profounder institutional and local turn. There are those who already think that the original destination of the Epistle was Rome. Thus the Epistle seems set for its Romanisation. If that be done, Plato as ancestor will have some altered features and wear a toga.

---

[1] *The Epistle of the Priesthood* (1913).
[2] *The Platonic Tradition in English Religious Thought* (1926).
[3] *Studiorum Ducem*, 29th April, 1923.

That Greek rather than Latin thought should rule the Epistle in later Europe has been due to Alexandria rather than Athens.[1] Philo is the spiritual ancestor of another large family. He sent Moses to walk the groves of the Academy with Plato. His Pentateuch was interleaved with excerpts from the writings of the Athenian philosopher. But how came he to have posterity among commentators on the Epistle ? Through the Reformation doctrine of the Bible. What, it may be asked, has Plato to do with any post-Lutheran thing ? Erasmus would appear to offer an open door for the passing through of the philosopher whose ideas and language have a sort of musical kinship. Yet it was not the scholar who edited the Greek New Testament that was sponsor to the philonic line. It was the theologian who framed a doctrine of the Bible so that it could be personalised and take the name *Logos* or the Word of God, which actually belonged to Jesus Christ. It will be remembered how round about the first century there was a movement in Jewish thought which passed almost imperceptibly from the idea of the Wisdom and Word as the creative agency of Jahwe to the idea of the Torah of Moses as that agent. The shift in thought personalised the Pentateuch. That is a parallel to what has been done in European thought. The Book insensibly took on personal qualities from an idea and name which was found to be both Greek and Hebrew. Philo had organised an intellectual union of the two on the basis of the platonic view of the Logos. The union of Old

---

[1] On Latin Fathers see Riggenbach, *Die Ältesten lateinischen Kommentare zum Hebräerbrief* (1907).

and New Testaments in the Bible was made to respond to the union of Hebrew and Greek things in the writings of the Alexandrian Plato. Exegetes in the Church of Rome have been his sons. Rohr[1] is an example. It is not difficult to cause Philo to walk in step with Augustine. Still the larger number is in the Reformed churches. They produce the completer philonians. Windisch[2] is an outstanding instance. He waves, so to say, the rod of Moses over the Christology of the Epistle. The document is now ready to be an appendix to Philo's *Life of Moses*. The doctrine of the Lord becomes another Moses who had learnt from Plato. You will notice that it was not the Lord Himself who thus assumes another personality. Windisch has followed Philo. He turned a doctrine of Moses into another Plato. The perfect philonians make Philo to be a Christian before Jesus Christ, and a platonised Old Testament to be more Christian than the Gospels. There can be no doubt that Philo is the famous ancestor of this branch of the family.

Studies as well as commentaries upon the Epistle make up the high road we are examining. It is not proposed, at this point, to trace the genealogy of the many studies. They have Plato or Philo as ancestor. The most recent of them admits that some questions are shaping themselves which may disturb the settled Roman quality of the high road. Purdy,[3] an American

[1] *Der Hebräerbrief* (*Die Heilige Schrift des Neuen Testaments*) (1916).
[2] *Der Hebräerbrief* (1913) : cf. *Die Frömmigkeit Philos* (1909).
[3] *The Purpose of the Epistle to the Hebrews in the Light of Recent Studies in Judaism* (*Amicitiæ Corolla*, J. R. Harris, 1933), 253 ff.

student of the Epistle, is the author of the latest study. He releases us from dealing genealogically with some studies because he reviews recent works on Judaism and in connexion with the Epistle. Thus questions have arisen in his mind. In general he ranges himself with Moffatt.[1] In particular, he develops personal views on the purpose of the Epistle. We are ignorant, he tells us, of " any group of readers whose teaching or practices would call forth such a masterly apology." We may perhaps never know who these were. That grey view is companioned with a second one. That perhaps the matter " cannot be better formulated than in Moffatt's answer."[2] What were its points ? The Epistle was written to those who were dominated by a " sense of disappointment " that the religion of the New Covenant " had no impressive ritual or an outward priesthood." For the writer himself " there could be no religion without a priest." His problem was theirs. Therefore he sets himself to bring out the " absolute value " of the priesthood and sacrifice of Jesus Christ. The Epistle is " no theological treatise." It organises its appeal on an " idealistic conception of the two spheres "—the real and the phenomenal. Shadow and substance, type and anti-type, make up a contrastive and cumulative demonstration of the superiority of the New over the Old Covenant. Till the Epistle, men and women were trying to find Jesus in the Greek Old Testament : a Christianity according to Septuagint proof-texts. Therefore, Moffatt represents the writer as pleading,

[1] Pp. xxv–xxvi.
[2] P. 254.

" Come back to your Bible, and see how fully it suggests the positive value of Jesus ! " Pentateuch and Psalter, the literature of tabernacle and temple ritual, are used " to illustrate the commanding position of Jesus Christ as the Son of God in the eternal διαθήκη." When all of his answer is most carefully weighed, this accomplished commentator is seen to be one of the Roman builders of the road. Patristic, Philonic and Reformation material are worked into the pleasant and erudite achievement which every student knows.

Purdy acclaims that answer. He does not assent to it. He writes,[1] for instance, " To be sure, Hebrews with its development of the Platonic ideas of substance and shadow, with its use of allegory, with its Melchizedek speculation, represents rather an heretical than an orthodox form of Jewish speculation." The first part is of the road ; the second part is off the road. He seems to have read back into the Epistle some later Melchizedekian heresy.[2] Further he holds that it will not be understood " unless or until we find evidence of a definite group of readers who correspond to the type of argument developed in Hebrews." We shall wait very long for them. They are as chimerical as the writer and Epistle. They and their first century may be found in a land somewhere beyond the cluster of the Pleiades. But the humane author of the Epistle was writing for the world of men and women.

The question which Purdy presents is to be found in his quieter rather than his more daring statements.

---

[1] P. 264.
[2] E.g., Hippolytus, *Philosophumena*, vii, 26 ; cf. Stork, *Historische Studien zum Hebräerbrief: Die sogennanten Melchisedekianer* (1928).

It is seen in this one : " Hebrews is much nearer current Judaism of the normative type than recent students have been accustomed to admit." Evidence of this is said to be in his argument about sacrifice— " the longest sustained argument in the New Testament on a single theme," so it is described. This current problem for Judaism is claimed as the main concern of the Epistle. " There is not the slightest evidence that the sacrificial legislation was side-tracked by normative Judaism."[1] Why Purdy could not rid himself of the term " normative " will soon be seen. For the moment, we have to recognise that his question is whether after all the Epistle is hebraic rather than hellenic. He admits the writer's " acquaintance with Philonic thought." Philo was, however, of Moses before he is of Plato. Purdy's pre-occupation with the problem of sacrifice points that though he may be of Philo he is indissolubly of Moses. This question then emerges : is the Epistle a wholly hebraic composition ?

For some students that question was answered a few years ago. The valuable compendium of Strack and Billerbeck[2] seemed to give an unfaltering affirmative. When their volumes are thought upon carefully another view is possible. The Epistle was sunk in an ocean of Jewish literature. Not a single passage had a chance of coming to the surface as a Christian statement against the load of parallels from Talmud and Targum. Its author became more hebraic than Moses. Philo seems an effeminate

[1] P. 262 ; cf. Bousset, Die Religion des Judentums (1926), 97 ff.
[2] Kommentar (1926), iii, 671 ff.

cosmopolitan by his side. Take the section of their book which deals with " High-priest and Sacrifice."[1] A transference of its values to the Epistle means not only the proof of Purdy's thesis ; but also the complete statement of the case that the New Testament was merely aberrant Talmud. It is hard to believe that students cannot see that such a transference must be made if the two documents are to be made alike. Another important thing to notice is that Strack and Billerbeck are almost all off and not of the road, and that Purdy joins them there with his question. Does this mean that when the Epistle is related with actual hebraic things its traditional treatment has to be left ? Will such a break mean that a more serious fracture has been made ? Is tradition truth ? Is the way of these last three writers the way of truth ? The emergence of such questions can be taken as a request for the rehandling of the Epistle.

This glance over the road of commentaries and studies leads to a broad conclusion and suggestion. The conclusion is : that a purely objective view of these works can be taken. They have been created, for the most part, by external influences. Platonism or Philonism have moulded the traditional interpretation of the Epistle. Purdy owes almost everything to the late Dr. G. F. Moore of Harvard.[2] Among the first words of the latter's book are these : " In the light of subsequent history the great achievement of these centuries was the creation of a normative type of Judaism." The centuries, we are told, are they " past

---

[1] iii, 696 ff.
[2] *Judaism* (1927), i, 1.

the middle of which the Christian era falls." Thus
Purdy's exemplary influence is manifest.   It gave him
also the word which gained control of his pen.   There
can be no doubt that Jewish literature of the extra-
biblical sort is the influence which created Strack and
Billerbeck.   Our broad objective conclusion must go
on to say that as external influences created the
commentaries, then tradition and its methods are due
to the same causes.   What of the commentary and
study which are off the road ?   As they are created by
external influences they could only set up another
tradition, if their ideas were followed by writers on the
Epistle.   Does that conclusion bring commentatorial
action to a standstill ?   On the contrary, it makes the
way free for the fresh internal handling of the Epistle.
It recognises too that discovery may produce such
instruments as will naturally evoke its meaning.

Therefore our prefatory suggestion is : that a sketch
of the general characteristics of the Epistle and its
writer can be drawn up which shall be true to its
internal evidence and also sensitive towards new
discovery for its interpretation.   It must not be made
in the light of any such discoveries.   Not so drawn as
to be hospitable designedly towards that evidence.   It
ought, indeed, to have no knowledge of what evidence
will be found.

To ensure these conditions the following account is
written solely from notes made several years ago.
Then the hope of other documents for the enlightening
of the Epistle was a very dim one.   Both writer and
Epistle are thought of as mind and expression swayed
by the Idea and the Person.   What is meant by those

terms will appear as we seek for the writer and why he wrote as he did.

A letter without a name can be like a lamp with no light. It is not alive. For the kindling flame in the signature is not there. That would be the condition of the *Epistle to the Hebrews* if the writer had not left us himself in the document. He cannot be named, but he can be known. The Epistle is a portrait of the man in the high moments of his thought. Its strokes are not forced. He is not bound to any artifice as he draws. That might happen to a sensitive writer, when he is trying to see and say certain things for others. Then a letter is only the distance of the strokes of a pen away from an essay or a treatise. Where no conscious art is used in the arranging of ideas, there the human being is in charge of the stylist. This man, whose portrait is his letter, was a sensitive writer. He wrote good Greek. But he wrote it for human nature's sake. His high moments of thought made him more sensitively human. He was not the thinker who had reached *there*. He was the man who saw with clear eyes how he, and the exiles to whom he was writing, could be drawn back to the paths which lay behind.[1]

For he was writing to the exiled mind. Each word of the Epistle is addressed to it. Whether they who had the Letter were also exiles in estate, we cannot say. It is natural to think in terms of foreign places when that word is used of men. The notion of exiles in estate may have to give way to that of exiles in spirit. His

---

[1] These reciprocities of spirit are not recognised by those who style the Epistle as being an " artificial " document, or who more carefully designate it a homily—*e.g.*, Slot, *De Letterkundige vorm van Den Briefe aan de Hebreën* (1912), 49 f.

Epistle could perhaps have been sent to dwellers in the next street. Since no phrase in it demands a geographical place of exile, we shall do well to recognise that he wrote to the exiled mind. It could turn its head to the Past in the guest he delighted to have at his table. The lure of the lowland ways was in his own mind. That others should not go back caused him to write his best Greek and his most solicitous thought.

To whom was he writing ? The shorter title of the Epistle informs us : *The Epistle to the Hebrews*. That scrap of external evidence is upheld by the contents of his Letter. The ideas are Hebrew ideas. They are of the kind which had haunted the mind of Israel since the time she began to weave those special dreams of hers which we call apocalypses.

The opening of the Epistle is an influential one. By its help we try to define through the use of certain powerful adjectives what sort of Hebrews the Epistle is addressed to. One of these adjectives comes from the name of a city, and the other from the name of a philosopher. We say then that the writer is moved to put Christianity in an Alexandrian form, or that his thought is philonic. The two adjectives make a tiny picture of what Alexandria and Philo, the famous Jewish writer, are said to be thinking of Jesus Christ and Moses towards the end of the first century. Thus the Epistle could be sent to any but Jews in the next street in Alexandria ; and the guest, who was welcomed by its writer, might be an inquirer of another race whose intellect viewed Jesus through the eyes of Philo—a thinker who looked at Moses with Plato's eyes. It seems as if such a view will demand some dexterity in handling a series of mental lenses. We must stop to make inquiries.

The first question which presents itself is : Would an Alexandrian Epistle[1] be likely to be found in the New Testament ? The book is composed of writings by some of the chief disciples of Jesus Christ. Epistles are sent to towns or peoples which had been evangelised by them. There is no true tradition that Alexandria was reached by one of His near followers during the first century. Paul cannot be made to bring it into the New Testament. Timothy could not have borne it from Rome. Thus, an Epistle written to or from Alexandria ought not to be found in the Book of Jesus Christ—unless the second question that arises can be answered in another fashion. It is : has an Epistle with what is called philonic Christianity been found in the New Testament ?

The door by which the Jewish writer is said to pass into the Epistle is made of these words : " the Son, whom he appointed heir of all things, through whom also he made worlds ; who being the Brightness of his glory, and the Image of his substance." That is supposed to be Alexandrian and not Hebrew architecture. Philo does use the terms Brightness and Image when writing about his own conception of the Logos or the divine Word. The first is a description of something this creative agency has done, and the

[1] The opinion of Eusebius, *Hist. Eccl.*, vi, 14, cannot make the document Alexandrian. Nor can the opinion which Luther popularised that Apollos was its author make it such, even though certain critics down to our own days maintain the view. It probably has no other basis than the Pauline saying : " I planted, Apollos watered " (1 Cor. iii, 6).

second describes that agency. Thus the human soul is said to be the Brightness of the creative word, because it is created in its likeness.[1] Whilst the Image is the likeness of Jahwe sealed upon his chosen one, the Word.[2]   What Philo is doing is this : he is trying to rewrite Genesis i, " Let us make man in our image, after our likeness," in the terms of Greek philosophy. He unites Moses and Plato.   The writer of the Epistle has as little interest in such an exercise as he had in calling Jesus the Logos. He did neither of these things. His doorway is not in the Alexandrian style.   To be that, its great feature would have to be—Jesus as the Logos. Philo's divine Word must have become joined with the Galilean, if philonic Christianity is to be found in the Epistle.   But Jesus is nowhere defined as the Logos by its writer. If that feature has to go, we can conclude that he had never been apprenticed to Philo.   S. Paul's Cathedral could not be the work of Wren, without its dome and pillared portico, any more than this Epistle might be in the philonic style without the Logos.

Perhaps, one will say, the Epistle looks in the direction of Philo's style—seeing that its writer could borrow his verbal architecture from the *Wisdom of Solomon* vii, 26 :[3] " She is the Brightness of the ever-lasting light . . . the Image of his goodness." The moves in thought which have to be made between that

[1] *E.g., De Opificio Mundi*, xlviii, 139, li, 146 ; *cf. De Fuga,* xxii, 110.

[2] *De Plantatione*, iii, 18 ; *cf. De Opificio*, vi, 25.

[3] There is no actual foundation for the idea of connexions between Philo and *Wisdom*. The opinion of Jerome that Philo was its author is without any support.

book and Philo are these : She is made into He ; the Wisdom becomes the Logos ; Jesus the Galilean is assimilated with the Hebrew idea of the Wisdom, and afterwards with the Greek idea of the Logos ; and finally, that Philo is somewhere an agent in this process of making Jesus from a person in a small country into an idea which could become a dweller in the mind of the wide world. This was done to make a small but beautiful ethic, which Galilee might realise, into a Christology which Europe should understand. Someone who was Hebrew was made, by the process of thought, into something that is Greek. There is, however, no historical warrant for such a view. The first century resists this way with itself. Its record is in the New Testament. That is the Book of Jesus Christ. Then it is He who resists our theories, because the book and the century have their meaning and order only as He is allowed to be Himself. The first century knew this, so that men and message and ministries, after the earthly work of Jesus had closed, are to be understood only in the light of the supremacy of Jesus Christ the Revealer and His revelation. Thus the unknown writer of the Epistle was one of these men. He could write Greek as Paul could not. He was not, therefore, a gifted thinker whom the Holy Spirit had raised up to transform the message and nature of Jesus by the help of Moses and Plato, as seen through the eyes of Philo. Nor was he chosen to clarify and complete the thought of Paul. He was a Jew whose mind was ruled by the Idea which was the great motive in his nation's religion, but he had become a disciple of Jesus Christ whose endeavour was to subdue that Idea to the Person and His revelation. The writer had to be an exile from the Idea that he might be at home with the Person. This is what discipleship to Jesus should mean throughout the ages. Let us trace further how an exile of the first century taught other exiles to become at home with Him. In this way we shall learn how he taught himself.

From verses two to four in the first chapter of the Epistle, the writer lightly paints in an impression of Jesus Christ. He is the Son who is the Brightness and the Image ; who upholds the scheme of things by the word of His power ; who sits at the Right Hand of the Majesty in high places and whose estate is higher than the angels. Jesus is painted in the tones of the Idea. The Person is certainly within those tones. He is robed in them. Are they from a Greek or a Roman palette ? An answer to that question will come, if a primary question be asked : What was the Idea with whose colours He is depicted ?

Let anybody take up one of the greater Hebrew apocalypses, and the palette is in his hand. We will suppose that the choice is the *Hebrew Book of Enoch*.[1] It can now be read and understood by those who have not the call to acquire any other language than English. This book is the Idea written in the form of vision for others to read. This is nearly all that an apocalypse means. What then is this haunting idea ? It was said that again and again Jahwe had chosen *the Man* to be his delegate on the earth. He gave him names which conferred those energies upon him by which the world is upheld. This chosen man also

[1] Odeberg, 3 *Enoch or the Hebrew Book of Enoch* (1928).

was Jahwe's creative agent. He alone of human beings partook of the Brightness of the Glory. Upon him was stamped the Image of Jahwe. He too was admitted where none other could come—to a place by the Right Hand of Jahwe. With it death and judgment were said to be dealt out to men. *The Man* set near to it was its elect executant. No angel could hold that place. And the end of this Idea was to establish on the earth a dominant state of Israel in which should be made perfect ritual worship of Jahwe. This dream informs the pages of the Old Testament. Its beauty has given us the apocalypses both within and without that venerable book.

No Greek colourist could have put a brushful of tint into that picture. It is as Hebrew as the Old Testament. The Idea, then, is not in the slightest stroke or tone a creation of Greek philosophy : it is in every hue and line the creation of Jewish apocalyptic. Jerusalem cradled the dream and its draftsmen. Athens could never have conceived the Idea ; and could scarcely raise an interested head even when Paul told her of the Person.

The writer of the Epistle thinks first of Jesus in the terms of the Idea. He had to do so ; for he was a Jew. It was the bright life of the thoughts which were natural to him. The Person also was exiling him from the Idea. He had been at home with the vision for very long : he had to find himself at home with the Reality. He had as well to help others erase the Idea with its faculty to evoke the feelings of exile in them. A double motive took him back to the Idea, and a double motive took him on to the Person. His own

C

Hebrew mind and the Hebrew minds of his friends made him go back ; whilst his own discipleship to Christ and theirs bade him go on to know *the Man* who was not a figure of dream. The idiom of his message, and the vehicle of his and their removal from the old to the new home of the mind, came by going back.

The double motive which takes him onwards is to have God in the vehicle with all His powers to transform the old idiom and practice of religion. The transit from the Idea to the Person is made only in that way. When exiles travel with Him they do not at first work at the grammar of the language used in the new land of the mind. He instils it into them as He transfigures the meanings of the dialect of the old land. His very presence does that. And when He takes familiar words upon His lips they open out with novel and lovely significance ; since He touches the ideas in them with fresh life and perspective. This is part of the miracle which Jesus was and worked. God thus revealed in Him can go into any vehicle which moved men to His own land of the mind—whether from old Jerusalem, or Athens, or Rome. We later folk who talk so much about the means of transport, forget the need for the presence of the Transfigurer. The writer of the Epistle could not forget Him ; for he knew that without Him none can go from the old lands to the land of God's mind, nor can any other be Physician to the plight of the exile enthralled by the lowland ways behind him.

He remembered these things, and rendered the Idea in the terms of the Person. He would have forgotten them had he put the Person in the terms of the Idea,

Then indeed he might have copied from Philo. Or what is more likely, he might have chosen a series of Old Testament passages and have made a single comment on them : " the one of whom these passages speak is Jesus."[1] It is not to be denied that in some places of his Epistle it looks as if he had almost said that. The hand which held the pen was the hand of a disciple to Jesus ; but sometimes the hand of the exile would close over it, and the strokes of the pen would not be firm. The places are few where the strokes waver. They at least speak to the human in us, as they spoke to the one who among his correspondents could go back. For they remind us that a messenger of Jesus in the great days, whether he wrote or spoke for Him, always remained a human being. He had to bring his human nature into subjection to Jesus Christ, and especially the mind which is the governor of his human self—even when he was writing down the record of His public life or sending an Epistle to the Romans. The greater part of the immortal message of the New Testament, especially when we read beyond the Gospels, is its evidence how men such as we are triumphed over their many attachments to the lowland ways and became the freed men of the revelation of God. Among them is the nameless writer of the *Epistle to the Hebrews*. He could never have ministered to the exiled mind if he had not won this freedom for himself.

There is therefore a highway being made, between

[1] It must be apparent to any careful reader that these citations were not ordinary prophetical proof-texts, nor were they *testimonia* of an anti-Judaic sort, such as are in, *e.g.*, the Cyprianic *Testimonia adversus Judæos* or the *Trypho* of Justin Martyr.

all old lands and the land of God's mind, where this
writer is putting the Idea in the terms of the Person.
He does this in such a manner that the exiles may say :
" It is no more a dream, an apocalypse that flies on the
wings of the years. It is actual and true. The old
familiar words say so ! " But first he had to achieve
that knowledge. He has had to make the ancient
idiom say new things in such a way that they seemed
to be saying old things. The Jew in him had to go to
school, that he might catch something of Jesus' silent
and simple art of recreating language and men. For
the most part, he has learnt his lesson so well, there is
literally but the breadth of a pen's stroke between the
belief that he has put the Person in the terms of the
Idea or he has put the Idea in the terms of the Person.
That delicate pen's breadth means, however, a world's
width of difference for the mind. If the former is
believed, the Revealer remains unknown ; whilst if the
latter is understood, He can do His work in him and us
of creating men for the new land of the mind. In a
final analysis, the former means that He is composed
merely of such stuff as dreams are made of ; and the
latter that He is the most significant Person in the world
for God revealed Himself in Him. The writer of the
Epistle threw all the power of his intellect into the
realisation of the Person who had overcome the Idea.

His endeavour is to be found in every word he wrote.
It is done, as best he could, after the manner of his
Lord. Thus the subtle transfiguration of ancient
things could be wrought in the minds of the exiles.
But it had to go on in him and them, if either was to
become at home in the new land. For him or them

Jesus could not be a relative of Ecclesiastes. The exile is at home when everything is new under the sun. He may not reconstruct the home he has left, and declare he has crossed from one pole to the other of the world of the mind. He would thus be an exile wherever he stayed. First must come the almost insensible invasion of his personality by the Person, and afterwards the earnest setting of the faculties of his personality to know the Transfigurer.

We modern people have a dim sense of exile, because we do not realise that we live and move in old-world thoughts and practices as did the people to whom the Epistle was sent. We therefore omit His work of transfiguration and the exile's passion to attain a knowledge of His revelation, when we think and write about that document. For us the Idea has merely grown up. It has found better expression. It is a matter of literary style with us or a grading in philosophy. The old idiom has but a richer vocabulary. Ancient ambits of feeling have their edges softened, and so for us are mysteriously enlarged. What we do not care for in ancient cults is dropped, that what we care for may receive new names and sanctions. The highlands for us are always the ends of the lowland ways. We think the ancient world and ourselves have sauntered into the land of the mind of God. The writer of the Epistle knew that men get there only as they toil onwards from the ways behind them.

Thus the *Epistle to the Hebrews* talks Hebrew in excellent Greek, but almost everywhere the infolded Hebrew is spoken with the " ideal " accents of Jesus Christ. Where it does not, the writer's trouble is with the more sensitive syntax of meaning. Quite humanly, he finds difficulty sometimes in saying just what God would have him say, because the ear of the disciple is not yet attuned with delicacy to the whole of His revelation.[1] His achievements show that he was on his way to become a master of the one language of religion. This is the standpoint from which to judge what he has written. Therefore when we turn back again to the words through which, it is said, Philo passed into the text of the Epistle ; we can be assured that not even his shadow had fallen on the doorway. The main problem for us is to guard against allowing as much influence as possible for everyone and everything else and as little influence as possible for Jesus Christ, in this supreme matter of moulding man's mind to know God. Since our attitude to Him looks often as if we thought that He had come to be simply a ductile something for individuals and institutions to use at their pleasure. The writer of the Epistle made none of these mistakes. He could not have got home, nor could he have led his exiled brethren home, if he had shut out the Transfigurer. The very way the exile has to travel is Jesus. This man and his document " see Jesus only." He alone, and in Himself, is the transfiguring Truth. And through Him alone come those recreative energies of God upon human personalities which make us men and women. *The Epistle to the Hebrews*, like the other writings in the Book of Jesus Christ, strove to tell only these superbly vital facts to other human beings. Therefore its writer

[1] It is surely an astonishing judgment when Dibelius, *Geschichte der Urchristliche Literatur*, ii, 49 ff., describes the Epistle as " artificial."

and theirs brought themselves and others home, from the many ancient lands of the Idea where men are baffled of life, to the Person in whom God is revealed. Surely the other name of this Epistle must be " A Letter Against the Lure of the Lowland Ways."

Those exiles ought to be attested by their presence in the Letter. And that view of the Letter be capable of test by at least one of its chief ideas. They are here. Also both are arraigned at the bar of the most solemn idea in the document. The writer has drawn the four chief types of exiles in pictures one verb long. One, " glide by " (ii, 1); two, " almost reached " (vi, 1); three, " stopped growing " (v, 11); four, " fell away " (vi, 6); borrow a convention from Bunyan, and put Mister before each of those descriptions—then the types of exiles over whom the writer watched take on life. They become Jewish types and universal types. They are portraits of men and women in the first century, and pictures of us all. The goal is God in Jesus Christ : those descriptive terms represent human beings with heads which can always be turned to the Past. The spineless ; the self-baffled ; the indocile and the Judas are not types peculiar to the century when Jesus came into the world. The rule of the Silent Voices, which is in our very nerve-structure, creates them day by day—where human beings yield to ideas and practices behind them and not to the call of the God of Life. There is the same situation in the first as in the twentieth century : the ghostly dynasty ruling our nerves and the accep- tance of God revealed in Jesus Christ who alone can dethrone them.

As an overcomer of the exiled mind, the writer has two great qualifications : he has a strong social sense and an austere moral sense. He never thinks of exiles and their weaknesses as " You "—a body of other human beings whom he must exhort. It is always " We " with him. So strong is his social sense that this enfolding first personal pronoun opens out, from around his contemporaries, to gather in the men and women of the ancient world who had gone on the quest for better truth before Jesus came. This sense of the other exiles did not sentimentalise his moral sense. Its vital depth and height are of course the counterparts of the moral depth and height of its companion-sense. When the moral sense draws its life from the revelation of Christ, then the social sense will take on something of His pastoral quality. The writer of the *Epistle to the Hebrews*, therefore, is one of the most sensitive and severe disciples in the New Testament.

" It is impossible to renew again unto repentance those who were once illumined—they having tasted of the supernal gift and of the excellent word of God and being made partners of the Holy Spirit and of the powers of the coming age—and then fell away ; for they crucify anew to themselves the Son of God."[1] The solemnity of the writer's words is caused by the sight of exiles from the ancient world going away from the Revealer and His revelation. His mind has the true disciple's carefulness. He knows that the exiled mind

[1] It is difficult to understand what commentators expect to determine by surrounding this passage with Philonic excerpts, *e.g.*, Moffatt, 77 f.

is not healed by moving from the old land of the mind
to a neutral zone, where much of the old in practice
may be mingled with a little of the new in idea. The
exile is not a freed man because he can repeat the
alphabet of the new language, and put all his thoughts
into the ancient dialect of " a teaching of ritual
washings, and of laying on of hands, and of
apocalyptical resurrection of the dead." This writer
realises the spell of the Silent Voices in them. The
very presence of the Revealer and the good tidings of
His revelation had superseded all such matters. He
has more lucidly seized that fact than other disciples
of the Lord, except the author of the *Apocalypse*.[1]
Each of them, according to his powers, had to go on to
know Him. It is this which accounts for the cross-
lights in the New Testament—the Light of Life is
dappled and muted by lights that come from the
ancient world and from men with their varied alliances,
both of temperament and training, who are emerging
from its " darkness." They were all of them exiles.
Their writings manifest how the Revealer released them
and their endeavours to release others. The New
Testament has little true sense until that is realised.

Therefore, the writer of the Epistle knows too much
of the tyranny of the Silent Voices to put Jesus into
any other vesture than His own. His correspondents
and himself are most real human beings. Both he and
they have need of the most immediate sense of the God
who can pour the life which renews into all the powers
of the human personality. Only through the word and

[1] See my forthcoming book, *Anthropology and " the
Apocalypse."*

person of Jesus is this done.   In the first century it was impossible to think of the exiled mind without evoking and invoking the Emancipator.   It was not the figure of a tradition which rose up.   No compound of memory and reverence was called upon.   Jesus had not come to add agony to the nostalgia of man for the Past.   No exile could gain home with such a Christ.   Both of them would die in the No-man's-land, where mingle the darkness of the old and the mirage of the new land. Without the Revealer man has only the Past to trek back to : he cannot go on to a mirage.   The solemn message of the *Epistle to the Hebrews* is this :   there are only the Silent Voices or Jesus Christ.   The first century rings with that alternative of life or death. By none is this put more vividly than the writer of the Epistle who says, that a human personality which yields to the Silent Voices crucifies afresh the Lord Jesus Christ.

CHAPTER II

FROM broad characterisation of the writer and of
the sort of humans to whom he was writing, we must
turn to the Epistle itself. A fresh study of it as a
document is the final demand of what we have done.
This too is the demand from what the commentators
have done. The beauty of our writer's style, which
gives his work outer harmony, goes with a curious
choice of the material he uses which gives his work
an inner lack of harmony. This is the impression
we ought to have of the Epistle on any of its extant
estimates, from ancient Alexandria to New York. They
have tried to make its argument run smoothly, and
it will not. For by their treatment of the Epistle it is
but a restless shift from this to that in his Old
Testament material. There is also passed into it a
sense of loose workmanship in the fitting together of
what has been borrowed. The ends of his pieces do
not meet. The joints are not neat. It is as if he had
set out to make a mosaic. Some parts of his design
are achieved ; others are but hinted at. The current
interpretations lend him an artifice of harmonious
achievement. They impose a theory on the Epistle.

It is said that the writer is doing something after both
Jesus and Philo. Or that he is setting out his Epistle
so as to throw into relief a doctrine of the sacrifice of
Jesus Christ. The finding of the secret of the inner
harmony of his work is given up for the stating of a
thesis. He is made to follow a writer who would
have kept him from his work of leading exiles home ;
or to proceed along the lines of a Christology[1] which
could have had no estate or intention of primacy in
design for his mind or writing. Is there, after all,
any true inner harmony in the Epistle ? Let a list
be made of the Old Testament passages used by the
writer, it will appear to show either deep-set
disharmony or rather vagrant allusiveness in his work.
Psalter or Pentateuch, he seems to use neither with a
thinker's care. His way does not look to be that of a
scholar who scatters his rich knowledge. This sense
of disorderly reference increases if the material is
examined in the various contexts it receives from the
writer. Thus viewed his Epistle does not build
itself up, as the commentators imply, in an inevitable
way. It does not march. It moves like the steps of
one of his exiles—some paces on the road ; some off
the road ; some in an aimless manner because his
eyes are on the old and his feet towards the new land ;
some with the high courage of deep belief in Jesus
Christ. From this point of view it is a very unhomiletic
homily.[2]

---

[1] *E.g.*, Streeter, *The Primitive Church* (1929), 194, who considers that the writer contrives " Christological doctrine " as a
bridge between Ephesians and the Fourth Gospel.

[2] *Cf.* F. Dibelius, *Der Verfasser des Hebräerbriefes* (1910), 13,
whose view demands technical order of arrangement.

This writer's mind is too sensitive that he should have designed the Epistle to imitate the exile who gets home somehow. Whether then the apparently wingless succession of Old Testament matter or the appearance of any one of his subjects as that which dominated him be considered, neither is capable of imparting inner harmony to the Epistle. His aim, however, was not artistic disorder. And any one of his subjects is an item in and not the whole of his scheme of ideas. There was some other compulsion upon this excellent stylist that he should use what he has from the Old Testament, and compose his document in the fashion he has, so as to bring himself and his exiles to another mountain than Sinai.

What made him do as he has done ? The beginnings of an answer can be found in chapter i. A direct way to evoke it will be to turn the affirmations of others into questions. They have helped to set up the Epistle's problem of disharmony. They should thus serve towards bringing back the true sense of its harmony. These questions are three. Was the writer of the Epistle merely a literal user of a certain Greek text of the Psalms ? Or was he citing it under theological control ? Or was he drawing upon a controversial *florilegium* of Old Testament passages ? First, it looks as if he had used an uncommon Greek text. His citation from the *Song of Moses :* " and let all the angels of God worship him," appears to settle the question. We know it as a Septuagint addition to Deuteronomy xxxii. What is not fully realised is that the *Song*, with this added stanza, appears in the Greek Old Testament as an appendix to the Psalter. Then the writer may

have cited it as a psalm and not as a pentateuchal
document. The final reason why it is found in the
Epistle is in its distinctive reading ἄγγελοι with *codex
A* instead of υἱοί with *codex R*.[1] Up to this point our
answer finds but small disagreement among recent
students of the Epistle. They will say, however, that
it does not go far enough. Not content with a
documentary answer they must have a theological
one. It is clear then that the Epistle must be tested to
see whether there was theological intent in the writer's
mind when he quoted the Psalter.

Robertson Smith,[2] for instance, said that there was
such intention. His short study has the edge,
brightness and potentialities of a short sword. A
characteristic piece of work which has had much
influence.[3] For him metaphysics and history organise
the opening of the Epistle. It is concerned with the
historic Jesus who becomes the exalted Christ. Two
wings of doctrine bore Him upwards : a doctrine of
angels and a doctrine of creation by the Wisdom of
God. The first Jesus surpasses : the second Jesus
assumes. The former gave Him superiority of office :
the second regality of activity. He is higher than the
angels ; and the Græco-Hebrew idea of a Sophia-
creator passes into the supposedly Christian conception
of " a place in the order and hierarchy of salvation."
It almost looks as if the man who took the name of

---

[1] König, *Das Deuteronomium* (1917), 207, dismisses the A
reading as "*falsch.*" A widespread view. But it does not
comprehend the Hebrews' usage of Deut. xxxii.

[2] *Christ and the Angels, Heb*. i, *Expositor* (1881), i, 25 ff.,
138 ff. ; ii, 418 ff.

[3] *E.g.*, An apposite illustration is found if Moffatt is compared
with Robertson Smith.

Dionysius the Areopagite had been called in to clothe the historic Jesus. These views organise the Epistle. They have ways also of informing its citations from the Old Testament. Two illustrations can be taken of what is thus done. First, the verse from the *Song of Moses*. Robertson Smith invades it and its original context so that the verse issues as having little or nothing to do with Jahvistic theophany, but as having all to do with a form of judgment which accompanies a second coming of Jesus Christ. Second, the citation from Psalm cx is treated so that it expresses nothing but a theological doctrine of the Messiah. It is a curious feature of this eminent Arabic scholar's work that he seems to be drawn towards neo-Platonic things and not to feel the pull of Semitic things. Moffatt is as hospitable towards late Greek things as he is, but with a difference. It is doubtful that he will go beyond Philo. He is more cautious in his handling of the contexts of the Old Testament material used in the Epistle. But he puts them within another context —" The Philonic atmosphere in which the eternal Now overshadowed the things of space and time."[1] Therein go the Epistle's chief ideas. It makes one wonder if somehow Thomas Carlyle had joined with Philo Judæus to produce both attitude and phrasing. Our second question must wait for its answer until the third one has been stated.

The work of a Dutch scholar[2] raises the third question. He considers that these citations come from

---

[1] *E.g.*, Moffatt, xliii and 9 ff.

[2] Plooij, *Studies in the Testimony Book* (*Verhandlingen der Koninklijke Akademie van Wetenschappen te Amsterdam, Afdeeling Letterkunde*, N.R., xxxii, 2, 1932), 31 ff.

a book which " sprang from the fiercest struggle of the new faith for its existence." This book he calls the *Testimony Book*—a title given to it before by certain British scholars.[1] Plooij considers it to be " the oldest written document reflecting controversies of the kind described in Acts vii–xxviii, 23 ff." Its title is not an original one, since it is borrowed from a well-known Cyprianic writing, *Testimonia adversus Judæos*. The Bishop of Carthage edits a small book of citations from the Old Testament which are so arranged under headings as to display the superiority of our Lord and of the Christian *cultus* over Jewish ideas and practices. Plooij uses another anti-Judaic text as the basis of his study upon the Epistle. It is a Latin dialogue between a Jew and a Christian. Harnack[2] showed that it had at least connexions by source with the second century ; therefore, a venerable document and of importance by reason of the material it embodied. The Dutch scholar takes its source farther back than that. He contends that it " was extant and in use in the primitive Aramaic-speaking church of Palestine."

The contention is that this dialogue and the opening chapter of the Epistle not only follow the same lines, but also draw upon the same source. We will, first, follow the argument without making comment. The Epistle speaks of the Son " through whom also he made the worlds " (i, 2) : the dialogue refers to Genesis i, 26 : " Jahwe said, come let us make man in our own image." Close upon its assertion, the Epistle cites Psalm ii, 7 : " Thou art my son, I

---

[1] *E.g.*, Harris and Burch, *Testimonies*, i and ii.
[2] *Texte und Untersuchungen*, i, ii (1883).

to-day have begotten thee." In like manner, the dialogue follows its Genesis citation with the same one from Psalm ii. The Jewish controversialist, however, declares that Jahwe made the Genesis statement concerning angels. Upon which his Christian opponent answers : " You are in error, Jew, for to which of the angels did he say, thou art my son." Up to this point it is claimed that the dialogue " completely corresponds with the text book on which Hebrews is drawing."

The Epistle then proceeds to cap its citation of Psalm ii with another from 2 Samuel vii, 14. The dialogue drops that one, because it is of another order of testimony than that which is required to demonstrate divine Sonship. Plooij calls it a temple testimony ; hence it would not be cited as a Sonship testimony. Following the Samuel citation, the Epistle goes on to link Psalm lxxxix, 27, for the title " First-born," with its distinctive quotation of Deuteronomy xxxii, 43.[1] The dialogue here reads : " again in the psalm he saith, I will make him *principem*." This title its author says the worshipping angels use for the Christ ; then he cites immediately the Deuteronomic Song, xxxii, 43. Plooij concludes that chapter i of the Epistle and the corresponding page of the dialogue " used what seems to be the opening chapter of the *Testimony Book* : On the Son the first-born of all creation." According to this view the writer of the Epistle was taking his Old Testament material from a controversial *florilegium*.

If now we work back from the third to the first question, we shall be able to gain the answers we seek.

---

[1] Note that the text of Deuteronomy as edited by Brooke and Maclean, *The Old Testament in Greek* (1917), i, 666, has this line.

D

The anti-Judaic solution is no answer. What is said in Hebrews i, 2 is not the equivalent of Genesis i, 26, nor will it be an echo of early controversy which centred about that passage. There can be no doubt that the phrase of Hebrews i, 2, which here is in question, is based on the same source as the whole of the verse which follows—that is upon Wisdom of Solomon vii.[1] The twenty-second verse of this chapter declares that the *Sophia* is " the artificer of all things " : a declaration which would naturally help to compose the Epistle's opening statement. Further, the critic draws together the texts of the Epistle and the dialogue much too closely when he disallows the latter's reading of *principem* in its citation of Psalm lxxxix. He extrudes that word peremptorily that he may conform the verse to Hebrews i, 6, and its use of the title " first-born." Jesus might be said by the author of the dialogue to have royal rank over the angels which is just what his argument affirms ; but He could not be said to be the " first-born " among them. The Christian in the dialogue wants to win his plea by orthodox statement and not to convert his Jewish interlocutor by heresy about the angels.

A larger consideration, even than important textual ones, appears to put aside the idea that Epistle and dialogue were drawing upon the same anti-Judaic source. A comparison of the two documents and their use of analogous material exhibits : first, that the Epistle's handling of argument and citation is original

---

[1] This, as will be shown, does not mean that in the first century a stage of Christological speculation can be labelled as Sapiential ; Windisch and Rendel Harris among others have maintained this view.

to itself and its author ; second, that the dialogue's
rehandling of both is conformed to the meeting of later
and rabbinised thought.   Whatever links the dialogue
can find with the anti-Judaic documents of Cyprian
and Lactantius,[1] and at those points where they quote
some of the same Old Testament material as the
Epistle : it is impossible to disbelieve that the dialogue
and they and their anti-Judaic original have the
Epistle only as their source.   Thus the third answer
casts us back upon the second question.   From an
anti-Judaic battery of proof-texts to the Old Testament
read in a theological way.

Now it is said that the writer of the Epistle is
probably organising his Old Testament material in
such a way as to meet " contemporary belief about
angels and revelation,"[2] though this intention does not
fully appear until chapter ii.   Meanwhile his citations
in chapter i are meant to explain, first, Jesus' " more
excellent name " ; and second, how He was " so
much better than the angels."   The citation of Psalm
ii, 7 in Hebrews i, 5 names Him as Son ; and the
string of citations in Hebrews i, 6 to 14 makes proof
of His estate.   The writer of the Epistle is not moved,
we must note, by any ideas of rank in divine agency.
His concern is with the " name."   What his Old
Testament material yields is not support for argumen-
tative doctrine but a series of names.   They are Son ;
Firstborn ; God ; Lord.   These are not all.   The
series goes on into the texture of his Epistle.   The

---

[1] The reasons for my findings are given in the text of this
book.
[2] Moffatt, 9 f.

second chapter yields two most necessary members :
Man ; Son of Man. The third chapter has just as
valuable ones : Apostle ; High-priest ; the Faithful
One. In other words, the Epistle to the Hebrews is
using the same material as John's *Apocalypse of Jesus
Christ.*[1] Both writings are talking apocalyptic. Neither
is arguing Christology. Both are transmuting Jewish
apocalyptic into Christian values by giving Jesus the
names which for so long have been borne by Jahwe's
" Sons of the Man."[2] The dreams of the greater Jewish
Festivals—of the reign of such a surrogate and the
establishment of a Jerusalem perfect in ritual faith—
—have been transcended in the historic Revealer and
His revelation. These great matters are put in the
only way by which they could reach the Semitic mind,
that is in the series of well-known names. They are
made His own ; thus the Semite could grasp the good
news of God in the very idiom of the Folk-mind. It
was not something brought home to him as if it had
been easily and well said. With gracious stealth the
old words instilled new truth into his mind, and made
him at home with itself. We ought rather to say,
Himself. The names with their ancient values stirred
the Folk-mind to think of such men as Moses and
Elijah and to dream of another in their line. The
same name with their new values wooed that mind to
the achieved revelation of God, because therein Jesus
was now the " Son of the Man."

It is of the utmost importance for the understanding
of the Epistle, and for the thought of the first century,

---

[1] i, 5, 8, 18.
[2] See once more my new book on the *Apocalypse*.

that we should realise aright this subject of the names.
That Old Testament and similar material supplied only
a series of them.   Not because the New came after the
Old Testament ; nor because the Idea simply trans-
ferred itself to the Person.   Those reasons will explain
factors in the thought of Augustine [1] and perhaps in the
attitude of Justin Martyr[2]—they do not account for the
ways of the revelation of God in Jesus Christ.   Thus
when we turn to those early Christian writers who,
through their source, have taken a part of their material
from the Epistle, it is essential to notice that we are
still dealing with names for Jesus and not doctrines
about Him.

The Cyprianic writing *Testimonies against the Jews* is
an outstanding instance.   The Hebrews material is in
its Book Two.   This Book is arranged in sections,
many of which are headed by a name for our Lord.
Under four of them will be found some of the citations
of the first chapter of the Epistle.   Under section i
is Psalm lxxxix, 27 : it is headed with names, Christ as
Firstborn and Wisdom.   Under section vi is Psalm
xlv, 6 and 7 : the name over it is, Christ as God.
Section viii has Psalm ii, 7 :   the name here is Son of
God.   And section xi has 2 Samuel vii, 14 to prove that
Jesus is of the seed of David.   Three citations do not
appear, Deuteronomy xxxii, 43 and Psalms cii, 25–27,
civ, 4.   The material from the Epistle appears among
a medley of Old Testament excerpts.   Stronger
language might be used of them, if we made the

---

[1] *E.g.*, the underlying suppositions of *De Civitate Dei*, Lib.
xv ff.

[2] *E.g.*, *Trypho*, xxxii ff.

mistake of applying to them a scholarly sense of context
and interpretation.   Such wild growth is but witness
to the fact that they were chosen for the sake of a name.
Let the sense of the verses be what they may, if they
contain the wanted name then they had a place in
early *anti-Judaica*. Without going farther afield in
this matter, we are able to conclude that the material
borrowed from the Epistle was for this reason and of
this nature : it had cited a series of passages because
they yielded a list of names for Jesus, which names
hitherto had been conferred on the man of Jahwe's
choice.

Another early text has been referred to, the *Divine
Institutes* of Lactantius.   His main source in Book
Four is very like that of Cyprian.[1] He disposes his
material in a less traditional manner.   The major facts
of the life of Jesus are set out in his gentle philosophical
way. He does not catalogue the names. His philosophy made him organise them.   It is done with
an almost untheological simplicity.   Still when his
book reaches its thirteenth chapter and he has occasion
to cite Psalm xlv, 6 and 7, he does so with this
comment, " by which word His name is shown forth."
Other citations from the Epistle are used by
Lactantius.[2] He omits some.   Deuteronomy xxxii is
the most notable instance.   Wherever the personality
of the writer may intrude itself as he handles the Old

---

[1] Further research into the sources of Lactantius has produced
substantial reasons for believing that he was drawing upon Greek
Anti-Judaica, which had conserved not only Old Testament
testimonia but also excerpts from the *Odes of Solomon*, Hermetica,
etc.

[2] *Div. Inst.*, iv, 8, Ps. civ, 4 ; iv, 12, 2 Samuel ; iv, 15,
Ps. ii, 7.

Testament material, or however his attractive philosophy may incline him to arrange it ; we can be sure that it came to him exhibiting solely a number of names for Jesus.   Lactantius and Cyprian, therefore, offer reflexive support to the view that the writer of the Epistle was as well using his material in the same manner ; since their source had taken its inspirative deposit from the Epistle.   We shall soon find other reasons for the opinion that our writer is original in this matter.   Whether the *Testimony Book* is behind the text of other New Testament writings is not a present problem.   Such a book may also have been the chief literary instrument in the early controversies between Christian and Jew.   One conclusion alone touches the Hebrews.   It is dependent on that Epistle for a portion of its contents and the Epistle is in nowise its inheritor.

One of the names for Jesus raises the question of the setting-out of the Greek text.   As it is usually printed the name *Prototokos* hardly catches the eye. The transit to the citation from Deuteronomy is thus too rapid.   We are scarcely given time to realise that the opening of verse 6 is as important as its reference to the Pentateuch.   It mingles the Idea and the Person : apocalyptic and history.   That is what the writer does elsewhere in his Epistle at the command of the Revealer.   Here it is done so as to weave a strand of its structure.   The opening of the verse is vitally connected with its citation of the *Song of Moses*.   We have gone on to an anti-Judaic text like the Cyprianic and have read back its proof-text for the name " Firstborn."   That is of course Psalm lxxxix, 27.

The late Dr. Briggs[1] showed that the lines of this Psalm which immediately precede this verse merely " paraphrase " Deuteronomy xxxii, 6 ff. That is not remarkable when we recall that the Talmud[2] tells us how this chapter was, first, the great Sabbatical canticle in the Temple and after in the services of the Synagogue. It was bound to beget songs. In Psalm lxxxix there is also the same link between the name Prototokos and Deuteronomy xxxii as in the Epistle. This does not mean that any extant text of the canticle has the name for Moses. There is no need to conjecture whether any lost text said that. We must become aware of what our writer and John the apocalyptist knew, namely, that in the first century a portion of Deuteronomy xxxii which was the *Song of Moses* became also his " Life."[3] Jahwe nurtured him when his mother had to abandon him. The name would fit such a son. By the side of these facts we should put another. In 4 Ezra vi, 58 and 59, the nation of Israel is personalised and given such names as Jahwe's firstborn and only-begotten and beloved. Those names had come to her, in the progress of apocalyptical thought, from the " Sons of the Man " whose greatest historic figure was Moses.[4] There is then no reason for going to Psalm lxxxix as the Epistle's source. That is a good analogue for later *anti-Judaica*

---

[1] *The Book of the Psalms* (1907), ii, 260.
[2] *Rosh Hashanah*, 31a.
[3] See my *Anthropology and the Apocalypse*.
[4] For the " Song " as a Psalm see, for example, James, *The Canterbury Psalter*, 1935, fol. 207b—the work of the scribe Eadmer in the twelfth century. He also pictures Moses as " Revealer." He puts him on a low mountain, speaking to crowds of men and women.

which on the whole were shy of extra-biblical references.
They do not utilise the seventh chapter of the Book of
Wisdom, for example, as does the writer of the Epistle ;
nor as we shall see had they his compelling reason for
doing so. He does not cite any testimony passages
for Prototokos. But he presents the historic fact of
God's bringing his Son into the world as affirmed by
words from the *Song* which contains an apocalyptical
" Life " of Moses. The writer has in mind the list of
names for the surrogate of Jahwe : he is thinking in the
terms of apocalyptic and is turning them into the
alphabet of the revelation of Jesus Christ that Semites
might understand Him.

The strand of structure woven from this name and
the *Song of Moses* shows itself in a nearby and unrecognised place. This time it introduces the names, Man
and Son of the Man, in chapter ii, 5. It reads, " For
not unto angels did he subject the coming world."
The oldest form of the text of Deuteronomy xxxii, 8,
says that the Highest appointed an angel over each of
the nations except the people of Jacob. The *Book of
Jubilees*[1] adds the interesting statement " to lead them
astray from Him." Whilst the Wisdom of Sirach[2]
renders the situation thus, " For every nation he
appointed an angel, But Israel is the Lord's portion :
whom he brought up as his firstborn with severity, yet
loving them." That reads like an under-text to the
situation in the Epistle i, 6 and ii, 5. It merely veils
the realism of *Jubilees* as did Deuteronomy xxxii. The
cosmos which was to come, what the writer of the

[1] Charles, ed. 1902, xv, 31, and note.
[2] xvii, 17.

Apocalypse of Jesus Christ calls " the new sky and earth," could not be entrusted to them. But to whom ? Hebrews at this point manifests that its writer had in mind an actual list of names with which to blend the *Song of Moses*. He wrote τὴν οἰκουμένην τὴν μέλλουσαν. His list contained this name, πατὴρ τοῦ μέλλοντος αἰῶνος—that is a list of the names of " a son " preserved by the first Isaiah.[1] It is plain that the bearer of this name would have the guardianship of the coming world. We must abstract it from the book and choral glory of Händel's oratorio. It ought to take on the earlier music of the Semitic Folk-saga of *the Man ;* and then to slip almost imperceptibly, as in the Epistle, into the later music of the Son of the Man in whom God revealed Himself. This Isaian list, so we shall find, was used again in brilliant style by the writer of the Epistle.

Therefore, our strand of structure is combined with a larger one which passes into the web of the whole. The apocalyptical names of the Idea are transmuted into names for the Person and by His revelation. Each of them should be picked out in heavy type to aid their becoming as significant for us as for the author of the Epistle. The pieces from the Old Testament are only chariots to bear those wearers of an immortal crown.

The Epistle goes on to speak of the One who crowned them. Or rather a picture is drawn of Him. It is not a full-length portrait. What is said in the first verses of the Epistle will have to be added to chapter ii, if we are to see Him as this artist saw Him. Let us remind

---

[1] ix, 6.

ourselves of the sort of artist he is. A Semite, who is a Christian and can write Greek, is working within the context and into the core of the ideas of the Semitic Folk-mind. Both the Idea and the Person govern his sense of colour ; but the Person controls his sense of line. Apocalyptic and history : the most familiar Semitic ideas and the revelation of Jesus Christ, are upon his palette. He paints, then, so that the Semite shall comprehend. History takes on some tones from Folk-ideas. Certain students have thought that he was working as a pupil of the Rabbis.[1] That he was taking the literal paradox in Psalm viii to prove that there was no such actual paradox in the life of Jesus. We have found, however, that the Psalm only yields for him those potent names, Man and Son of the Man. In causing the Revealer to crown them, the writer was trying to give Him natural access to the Semitic mind. Those names evoked its cherished dreams. He would have it understood that they now were abiding achievements. Hence he must follow the problems those dreams would inevitably present. They would say : if there is no longer the Idea but only the Person, why does He die ? The angels of the Idea do not die. The dreams at first would only see that the Son of the Man died as they and their dreamers die. But the writer is a disciple of the Person. Whatever apocalyptic has to make of " higher " and " lower," the revelation has to demonstrate its most potent historicity. The Lord died to overthrow Death—that personalisation of the principal ideas of apocalyptic and their effects in human personality. His Son of the Man is pictured

---

[1] *E.g.*, Robertson Smith, i, 138 f.

as doing just that.   The writer of the *Apocalypse*[1] did
the same.   Thus the historical Person and the details
of His history are so viewed that Semites might grasp
His truth and theirs.

It should be noticed too that the picture of Jesus
Christ is painted for the mind which could exile itself
from Him.   Both opening and closing verses of
chapter ii make this clear.   The opening ones depict
men who can be tempted into confessional unfealty :
the closing one etches in the Son of the Man who
could be tempted to the same profound disloyalty
towards His own *raison d'être*.   Our artist is drawing
his picture within that area of ideas.   He could not
have worked to the design of any theological doctrine
of the Humiliation of Jesus Christ.   Neither the Idea
nor the Person would require that of him.   We forget
their requirements.   It was impossible for him to do so.
When they are forgotten his picture gets out of drawing.
Then any Semite would have difficulty in grasping its
meaning.   And that would have defeated his art and
his Lord.

The classical manner with chapter ii composes a
grandiose and reverent picture.   The late Dr.
A. B. Bruce,[2] for example, painted one with a master's
brush.   But a Semite of the first century would have
had trouble with it.   He could not have found its
identity with chapter ii.   We have a precocity which he
had not.   The long influence of theology in Europe
has schooled our eyes.   Yet this picture, which is the

---

[1] I must again refer readers to the fresh discoveries in my
book on the *Apocalypse*.
[2] *The Humiliation of Christ* (1876), 32 ff.

heir of a thousand years' growth in doctrinal technique, cannot be put between the chapters of the Epistle without forcing the truth upon more careful eyes that it is foreign to the text. The blending of the colours of the Idea and the Person, and the use of them according to the technique of the revelation of the Person, will paint a picture of the Son of the Man who can deliver men from the fear of the place of the dead. It will show Him as the conqueror of the menaces from ancient Semitic cult and cosmical ideas. These shackled the personalities of lowly men and women so that they could not attain fullness of life. The view of Jesus which gave them liberty is what the Epistle depicts. High doctrine about His life and death would not reach down there. There can be no doubt that the writer was bringing a real deliverer to real men and women.

His handling of the subjects of disloyalty and sin throws that figure into relief. Concerning the first of these we are apt to overlook a simple psychological fact : the nature of the temptation to unfealty was the same for lowly men and women as for Jesus Christ. That fact filled the writer's mind. He had to bring his exiles home. To win them from the spell of the lowland ways. Was the Jesus of this Epistle then in bondage to the " silent voices of the dead " ?

The temptable Christ has become a part of the received picture of Jesus Christ. The first three Gospels are strained to produce the man who could be tempted ; and the fourth Gospel is put aside as history because it cannot be manipulated to that end. The irrelevant and irreverent imaginations of romantics have gone so far as to create a Jesus who came into the world to escape narrowly the breaking of Mosaic Law. It of course would have been no novel message from God to show others that hands can be kept out of neighbours' pockets and off their wives. A mind that is careful towards God and man could never discover what efficacy could have been His, if He had been tempted in such points. A temptable Christ, of the sort who might break either or all of the points of the Decalogue, is the creation of crude sentimentalism. This is a potent but unrecognised factor in much old and new theological speculation on this subject.[1]

Even the men for whom the Epistle was written are not tempted to the fracture of this or that maxim of Moses : they are tempted to disloyalty towards Jesus Christ the Revealer.   It is historic also that temptations were offered Him to deflect Him from the way of His revelation. The Temptations narrative admirably summarises that fact.   It appears again and again in the Gospels.   We seem to have lost sight of such features ; and cause a Jesus, whom we call human, to hurry on to His tragic crisis because our theological desire unites with our imagination to reduce Him to a formula of sacrifice.   The writer of the Epistle could not do that because of his most lucid and real idea of sin.

For the moment we have to glance onwards in the Epistle to the declaration about those exiles who crucify the Lord afresh. They have yielded to temptation. The results of sin are most austerely put. Indeed, the writer raises the question whether here the shadow-

[1] It is as well a dangerous strand in the received arguments for the Synoptic Jesus.

less brilliance of his vision has not carried his judgment beyond the more pitiful insight of the Lord's parable of the Prodigal Son.   Be that as it may, we can make no mistake if we unite his view of temptation and sin in the simple formula : Jesus Christ could have crucified Himself.   He could have yielded to the call of political power ; or have drifted back upon the lowland ways of religion.   He might have denied His own revelation for which the ancient world crucified Him.

This writer's vital idea of a Jesus who could be tempted as history tells us, then, was balanced by as vital an idea of sin.   A man sinned who did not believe in the Revealer and His revelation.   His sins were forgiven who believed in Him and it.   This change was not brought about by going from one school to another, from Moses to Jesus.   A rivalry of cults can alter little or nothing in human personality.   An upward progress of cults can alter little else than social manners.   God was and is revealed in Jesus Christ. Therefore the turning round of the mind to Him, from any of the religions of man, meant that human beings had willed to live in all the powers of their personality. To turn away from Him is to die away.   Men remain in sin who will not rise up to become His disciples. To turn from God or to resist or reject Him is sin.   This fracture is from the Life and not of ethical rules.

Thus the view of the first century that it was sinful, and led on to sins, to abide in the context of any of the religions of the ancient world—was not a polemic ; but a declaration of the degenerescence of man's being

in any other context than that of the God of Life.[1]
The criterion of sin could not be the breaking of this or
that social law, but the manifold flouting of Life in God.
Its motion could not have sprung from any act in a
garden, whose trees and fruit had known no other air
and sun than could be found in Semitic cosmology and
poetry ; but in the will of each man and woman set to
obey either the Silent Voices or God.

Therefore, instead of disharmony there is profound
harmony in the Epistle. The lists of names for the
Lord ; His picture ; the exiles and the meeting of their
case just where the lowland ways wove their magic and
the upward ways called to timid spirits—these are
intimate parts of the planned structure of the document.
Neither philonic nor rabbinic views of its exegesis can
yield this harmony. Since, so far as we have gone in
our examination of the Epistle, we have to find that
confusion must reign until it is learnt that its writer is
working upon an actual list of names for Jesus Christ.[2]
This is our first hint that he is basing his work upon
documents. And our first glimpse of the fact that the
list and its contents pass into the structure of the whole
Epistle. Moreover, they are the prefatory controls for
it and for us by which the significance of the Lord who
can be Life and Home to the exile is evoked.

---

[1] Much closer attention ought to be given to this view in any
attempt to assess a Johannine and Synoptic body of religious
thought.

[2] The question of this list is developed *infra, c. iii ff.*

CHAPTER III

A SIGN has emerged that the Epistle is shaped by documents and not by theories. That its writer is concerned with these and their transmutation, from what is Jewish into that which is Christian, rather than with essays in Christology. It is suggested too that his documentary base will have the most vital connexions with the deepest things of the Semitic mind. He is not a literary man. The artist in him is subject to his discipleship to Jesus Christ. That is not the formula of necessary convention for a New Testament writer. In the instance of our author it is the dual-mark of his service. He has been an exile from the Idea and is now at home with the Person ; and his art is set to minister to all who find it hard to resist the magic of the lowland ways behind them. His documents will have been formed by their spell ; and his healing by their transfiguration.

Two facets of this sign have so far appeared. An actual list of names for *the Man* of Jahwe ; and an actual chain of Old Testament passages which yield some names for Jesus Christ. The first has given little evidence of itself. The second could be the

E

result of arbitrary thought. Such critical suggestions can be extended. The list looks as if the Epistle had used it merely to enlarge it. The excerpts as if they might go on without number.

It will be well to remind ourselves that as yet we have gone but a short way with the Epistle. Those points of criticism which have just been made appear to be anticipated by the Epistle. The literal reference to the Isaian list breaks off where Psalm viii intrudes with the names, Man and Son of the Man. Is this textual fact also the Epistle's textual criticism of the sign ? It seems at first a natural inclination to say that those two names are not in the list. That, of course, is literally true. Our judgment of the letter involves another of the writer. He becomes a seeker after pieces from the Old Testament as one who searches for literal proofs to his statements. Whereas the Isaian list is an epitome of Jewish apocalyptic. The names are the gathering-points of its drama and ideas. Therefore the names Man and Son of the Man are implicit in all the explicit ones. For the Semitic mind, only Jahwe's Man can bear them. His dignity is also his essential name. Again, we modern folk have to release ourselves and those names from the charm of Händel's music. We have to listen to them as they sounded to Semitic ears. For them they made up the music, both tragic and triumphant, which accompanied their treasured dreams. These names were the heart and vision of apocalyptic—a much older matter than any messianic idea.

Does this view mean that the writer of the Epistle has the unlimited world of apocalyptic in which to move ? That he knows no documentary limit ? The simplest answer to these questions is that he would have used neither Isaiah vi nor the catena from Psalter and Pentateuch if he had not been under documentary control. The rest of our work on the Epistle will prove the rightness of that answer. At the moment it raises two most important considerations. First, that there was such a literal authority in the first century.[1] Second, that Isaiah vi was in such a context as could influence the writer's choice of Old Testament excerpts and contribute to the total structure of the Epistle. The treasury of apocalyptic was the Lectionary of the Synagogue, whose earliest strata have much longer history than the first century of the Christian era. Therein was our writer's literal authority. What was its power over him and what power it brought to his pen we shall find as we locate the Isaian list in the Lectionary.

Isaiah ix, 5 and 6, is the closing portion of the reading from the Prophets for the fourth Sabbath in Shebat, that is the eleventh month of the Jewish year. The day is an ordinary one. It is not a *red* day in the calendar. Its only festal distinction is that it follows, within a week, the New Year's Day for Trees.[2] That too is a distinction of the second grade. Since the festival has had little honour for many centuries, until its recent revival in Palestine. Twentieth-century reverences do not lend fame to first-century practices.

[1] Büchler, *The Triennial Reading of the Law and Prophets*, *Jewish Quarterly Review*, 1893, 420 ff. ; 1894, 1 ff.

[2] *Rosh Hashanah*, i, 1 ; *cf.* Surenhusius, *Mischna*, 1798, i, 301 ff., where the commentators discuss only questions of time and tithes.

They make no reason why the writer of the Epistle should have singled out an inconspicuous Sabbath. It may seem from all this as if such a choice ought to lead to the opinion that his was a fortuitous handling of the Lectionary. A case of the sort might be made out, if there were not three excellent reasons why the writer had himself chosen the fourth Sabbath of Shebat and not us. They are historical, ritual and literary reasons. There is nothing of chance in them, for they are of the marrow of the Epistle. But what history could make the undistinguished day distinguished ? There is no record of memories clinging to this Sabbath in a year's worship. The writer chose it because it was a day in a Maccabean month. In the month Shebat, Simon and Mattathias and Judas with their servants were treacherously put to death at a banquet by Ptolemy, son of Abubas.[1] A Maccabean factor in the Epistle has been suspected for a very long time. We shall be able to prove its deep and wide influence. For the moment, it is enough to claim that we have found the historical reason why this Sabbath was chosen.

What ritual reason could there be for its use ? The Epistle is not interested in trees ; and it is plain that the fourth Sabbath paid as little regard to them. This question is already answered in part. The Isaian list is among its lections. There was, however, more than this in its ritual material for our writer. We should note its characteristics. The Torah material is almost identical with that of the major festival of the giving of the Law. This fact singled out for him the fourth Sabbath. He needed its Torah material for the body of

[1] 1 Macc. xvi, 11 ff.

his Epistle, as we shall see. Whilst its prophetical material is for him, both literal authority, selector of other material akin with itself and vital link with Jewish apocalyptic. The Maccabean factor coalesces with more than one ritual reason why this particular Sabbath in Shebat should have been chosen.

His final reason is a literary one. Could we excise from the Epistle all that its writer owes to this entry in the Lectionary of the Synagogue, we should achieve something like a very fragmentary papyrus copy of that document. The bits could be labelled with its name. They would be authentic. But with its bulk the vital energy of sense has left the document. There can be no hesitation in thus highly appraising the influence of this Shebat material upon the matter, lively progress of thought and structure of the Epistle. These too are features which have yet to be brought into relief. Our first duty is to return to the subject of the connexions between the prophetical readings and the list of names from Psalter and Pentateuch.

A comparison of the list of names found in chapters i and ii with those in Isaiah ix, 5 and 6, exhibits some interesting results. The names are identical. Those which seem to offend theologians, who are more eager to get the late logic of their doctrine right than to understand the apocalyptical values of the names, are attested. Some names are not in the Isaian list. Prototokos is an instance. The Son of whom Isaiah speaks must of necessity have been the " Firstborn." The name could never have been Israel's as we have seen, nor given apocalyptically to Jacob[1] as other

[1] *E.g., Hebrew Enoch,* xliv, 10.

evidence shows, unless it had been borne by the Man of Jahwe. From his names other surrogates for Jahwe were named. Isaiah is heralding one of the line. We can be sure that he had this name. In like manner the names, Man and Son of the Man, are incontestably present where that Son is. He could have neither biological nor apocalyptical origin without them.

Further, an examination of the rest of the prophetical reading for the fourth Sabbath in Shebat—namely, Isaiah vi, 1 to vii, 6, manifests that there we have the inspiration for the other features in the first two chapters of the Hebrews. The throne; the worshipping angels; the earth invaded with glory and issuing from the divine person—these all unite with the Isaian names to aid the creation of the picture of the Son upon whose shoulders indeed the government rests.

The writer is not transferring material to his document but transmuting material for its composition. It is to be noted too that this does not mean an exercise of the imagination. He is not gathering facts of history and figures of speech and fusing those afresh in the fires of a mind which is of the poetic type. The change which goes on is more than a lyrical one. The man himself is as much in the power of the transmuting agency as is the stuff of his mind. We must become vividly aware of that fact. Our writer fundamentally goes to a non-biblical authority for his material. The Lectionary of the Synagogue is that authority. This we shall see as we proceed with our study of the Epistle. Though it is composed of pieces from the Old Testament, it is the conservator of the primary motions of the Semitic Folk-mind. Its material passes into the Epistle after it has been transmuted by the revelation of Jesus Christ. Thus we have already come upon a fundamental of the Epistle's structure. Its author is not passing material from the Old Testament into his document. He is inweaving such material into the Epistle from a non-biblical source after that it has been transfigured. The notion of transference is easy with the first method. It is difficult with the second mode. The theological aid which plenteously went with the former is not available for the latter. We shall do well to grasp this fact of a non-biblical source, if only for the reason that it will throw into sharp relief the greater fact of the control of the revelation of Jesus Christ.

What of the Torah lections on this Sabbath in Shebat ? Do they play any part in the Epistle ? Or have we the added problem of its writer's selective mind ? That would be a problem outside the control of any documentary source. He would choose according to the wayward quality we know as taste ; and he would not be the chosen penman of document and event. It is the latter situation, happily, in the Epistle and not the former. The writer is chosen, and what chooses him makes itself clear. We have seen already that these Torah lections were among the chief reasons why the writer uses their Sabbath in Shebat. His sense of artistry has determined, therefore, a place for them in the creation of his Epistle. These Torah readings were Exodus xviii, xix and xx. They cover the narrative of Jethro and Moses ; the Sinai theophany and a statement of Sinai logia. A first glance over them will register the opinion that those chapters have little verbal place in the Epistle. But such material can also give structural help. The figure of Moses, for instance, is a great factor in the Epistle. He must have had his source. We have realised that there are reasons why we cannot say, " of course that source was the Pentateuch." The Sinai theophany too is a dominating structural element. It manifests itself in the magnificent climax of the Epistle, where the contrasted peaks of Sinai and Zion take on respectively the shadow of the superseded and the glory of the abiding Christophany. Whence came these structural agents into the Epistle ?

A notable answer has recently been given to this question by a Dutch scholar.[1] He considers that one of the fundamentals of early Christian thought was the conception of the New Temple which should displace the Old Temple. It was designedly anti-Judaic ; and as such has passed into early Latin[2] and Greek[3] and Syriac[4] writers. This scholar believes that the conception was original to the controversial *florilegium* to which reference has already been made, and that it passed from thence into the pages of the New Testament. Therefore those writers were drawing upon a New Testament source and not upon the book itself. Now it is a feature of their statement of this conception that they constantly speak of the " House and Temple of God "—*domus et templum dei*. This double designation is derived from the " testimonium,"

---

[1] Plooij, 34 ff.
[2] *E.g.*, Cyprianic *Testimonia*, i, xv ; Lactantius, *Div. Inst.*, iv, 13.
[3] *Dialogue of Timothy and Aquila* (ed. Conybeare, 1898), 73 f.
[4] Aphrahat (ed. Parisot, *Patr. Or.*, i), i, 9 ; ii, 121, etc.

2 Samuel vii. That is an unmistakable textual feature.
We all know what play is made in the Epistle with the
word " House." Moses and it and Jesus Christ and it
are striking patterns set over against one another. It
is contended, therefore, that these were born of *anti-
Judaica* older than the Epistle. That Moses and Jesus
the High-Priest are conceptually derived from that
controversial source. They both stand at the entrances
to temples not made by hands but by words. They
do not belong to history but to argument. Polemic has
built from 2 Samuel vii two rival Houses and projected
two rival Servants ; and from these much of the
Epistle has taken shape.

This answer yields a non-biblical source for our
writer's service, if it could be shown that it was before
his time. That its verbal influence is almost negligible
is apparent. The Epistle uses the term House.
Nowhere is found the word Temple. It makes no
appearance even in the climax of the Epistle. Further,
the basic " testimonium," 2 Samuel vii, is not only
foreign to the Epistle, it is one which has been fitted to
an earlier series of Christian ideas that they and it might
become polemical instruments. There is no available
literary test which can demonstrate that these positions
should be reversed. Hebrews is before any *Testimonia
adversus Judæos* containing ideas analogous with its own.
Its subjects are original in their expression. They can
also be shown to have their own sources. We must
recognise as well that the use of such a source would be
outside the twin-inspirations of the writer. He is at
work within the radii of apocalyptic and history. The
documents of the Idea and the life of the Person

circumscribe his activities as thinker and writer. Where in these areas go the Torah lessons of Shebat ?

It has been said already that the writer needed this material. This as one of the reasons for his choice of the fourth Sabbath in Shebat still stands. We shall find that our next step in the investigation of his sources brings us to a more commanding series of lections from the Jewish Year, and that these ruled his choice of this particular Sabbath. Its Torah readings then blend with those more regnant portions of the Lectionary. They are not absorbed by them. The place given to Exodus xix in the triumphant " we are not come . . . we are come " of Hebrews xii, is more than sufficient to prove that claim. Other portions of the synagogal Lectionary may bulk larger in the letter of the Epistle : Shebat has a potent place in the structure of the Epistle from its beginning to its end. Just as its prophetical readings have deeply influenced the writer's choice of Old Testament material for chapters i and ii, so also its Torah readings have exercised the same power in other chapters. The Jeremiah citation, xxxi, 31 to 34, in chapters viii and x, is there not because the writer knew that on the Second Day of the New Year was read Jeremiah xxxi, 2 to 20 ; but because the prophet had in mind Exodus xix when composing the cited portion of his thirty-first chapter.[1] There are other instances of this sort of choice in the Epistle. They are not marks of scholarship. Nor had the writer Hatch and Redpath's *Concordance* at his elbow. The material of the Festal Calendar governed him. So

---

[1] We have not finished with the influence of Shebat in the Epistle as Chapter V of this study shows.

that he was inevitably guided in his linking up of matter analogous with its contents. A very sensitive mind moved by a profound anxiety which was working upon a small documentary basis, is the bald formula for the production of the Epistle to the Hebrews. To achieve this end, however, the formula must find the right and exquisite personality and there integrate itself.

Thus the Epistle makes no vagrant use of the Lectionary. Its ministry to the exiled mind dictated tender care in the shaping of its structure. There can be no doubt that the better half of such a document's structure is the selection of the sources whence it germinates. That our writer had these most sensitive gifts is proved by his choice of the fourth Sabbath in Shebat. Source and structure and style have that unity which must cause a critic to say : it looks as if the Lectionary material and sequent structure had chosen him. This impression grows as we trace out the tendrils of his design. It has the delicate strength of a plant as we follow root and leaf and flower from the major Lectionary influence ; the Melchizedek and Maccabean factors. Neither of these is engrafted on the others. The three break into the lovely and single flower of the Epistle. The whole is a triumph of the highest order of craftsmanship. It nowhere yields to the thematic architecture of the literary schools : it everywhere is shaped by an uncommon human being who had been schooled in the ancient Semitic world and in the new world of Jesus Christ.

CHAPTER IV

THE JEWISH CATASTROPHE AND THE MAIN HEBREW SOURCES OF THE EPISTLE

THE opening verses of the Epistle are generally described as its prologue. In practice its first two chapters are used as a prologue to its supposed chief concerns. The description arose from an erroneous parallel made between those verses and the first chapter of S. John's Gospel. The practice was created by the pre-supposition that the writer was elaborating either a doctrine of sacrifice or a statement of Christology based on new views of priesthood and sacrifice. A congruous documentary foundation for the whole Epistle naturally annuls both such views. But before we can go on to that subject, it is imperative for us to examine once more the Christological way with the Epistle. This can be done by the help of a recent restatement.[1] It has more importance than its own worth ; because its enables us to see clearly how and why that method has gained fresh mastery over the Epistle. Thus also can be learnt anew a large part of the reasons why it is necessary to lay bare the documents on which the writer was

[1] Wenschkewitz, *Die Spiritualisierung der Kultusbegriffe ; Tempel, Priester und Opfer im Neuen Testament* (1932).

at work. And the reasons will emerge for the presence of Sapiential material in the beginning of the Epistle.

This restatement says that one of the primary endeavours of the Bible is to give developing expression to the conceptions of temple, priest and sacrifice. They move from lower to higher views of themselves. At first this would seem to be a commonplace of to-day's opinions. Popular ideas of evolution and from the historical study of religions are its vocal parents. These generalisations have found their way into many learned books. Some phases of prophetic work and certain of the prophets may be illuminated by them. But Wenschkewitz is not content with that. He desires to demonstrate that this process of spiritualisation is the New Testament's main effort ; and that its work is illustrated chiefly in the book's presentation of Jesus Christ. He does not control the process : it controls Him. The movement began long before His time. He is its final result.

Thus, for example, the resultant in Ezekiel moves on through the Wisdom of Sirach, the Letter of Aristeas, the writings of Josephus to the books of the New Testament. It is a Palestinian process. The influences which lend it impetus are also Palestinian. There is no loop-like action on its part, in the first century, so that Alexandria shall be included as a creative factor.[1] It goes on from Hebrew things in Hebrew to Hebrew things in Greek. From the ideas of the Semitic Folkmind given a first expression, that is in Jewish

---

[1] Contrast, *e.g.*, Holtzmann, *Biblische Theologie des Neuen Testaments* (1911), ii, 334, makes the writer of the Hebrews a student of Philo's writings and attempts to trace verbal influences in the Epistle.

apocalypses, to those ideas given a second expression, that is in the New Testament. From books in which ideas had native dress for at-home life ; to books in which the same ideas have Græco-Hebrew dress for life in the great world. Nothing has undergone a " sea-change." Everything has merely grown-up.

This view, then, puts the material cited in the Epistle to school to an upward development of Hebraic things. Psalter, Pentateuch and Prophets are already in Greek. They have made the linguistic step upwards. The ideological step is naturally taken when they find themselves in Christian Greek documents of the first century. They have not come into a context which invades them. They invade the context in which they find themselves. It is in fact their creation. Jesus is there because of this material. It is not there because He has come. Psalter, Pentateuch and Prophets lend Him connotations. The life which causes a figure in a book to have ideas and motion comes from them. He is and speaks and does as they will. He is a someone who is written up into a something which is supposed to be the developing thought of Judaism. The shadow of an historic individual is given the substance of a doctrine, which has evolved through putting the Temple and its worship from an earthly into an apocalyptical sphere.

Now this new mode is an old one in a more subtle form. It used to be known as the typological way with the Bible. That was when theology stated the proposition of a Messiah in Genesis i and completed his demonstration in Apocalypse xxii. The ordered advance of the Semitic mind takes his place as the reigning fact in Israelitish religion. Therefore, Jesus

Christ becomes the last Man of Jahwe not by the aid of Augustine or Plato, but as the residuum of Semitic apocalypticism—the deposit clarified by the work of the centuries. He came to be not Himself but itself.

The idea of an upward spiritualisation of the features of Temple worship has, however, no place in history or literature. It certainly is not found in the evidence for Jewish apocalyptic. Ezekiel may dream of a new Jerusalem ; but there are conceptions and ways in his writings which are more primitive than those in the Book of Genesis.[1] John the apocalyptist is a New Testament writer. His consummate knowledge and use of the Tradition of Jewish apocalyptic make him contemporary with the first formulation of this fundamental of the Semitic Folk-mind.[2] When we examine those two outstanding writers more closely as spiritualisers, we shall find that they rebut the idea of the movement even with more force than those two estimates. Ezekiel nowhere spiritualises apocalyptic : he ritually reorganises it. John totally transmuted it. Ezekiel achieved by stripping away accretions from the old Northern cult conceptions : John by submitting them all to the revelation of Jesus Christ. Some Jewish apocalypses do etherealise the factors of apocalyptic. This was done by trying to release them from the swift circling of the ritual year ; by finding a resting-place for the dreams which would not come

---

[1] *Cf.* Perry, *Journal of the Manchester and Oriental Society* (1923), x, 51. This anthropologist has seized the important point, but his view of " archaic civilisation " is too general and his opinions on biblical literature are too obedient to that generality.

[2] See again my book, *Anthropology and the Apocalypse.*

true in the idea of a Moses who would come again, and by putting the whole apocalyptical scheme more and more in the sky. To spiritualise is not a change of site from the earth to the sky ; nor a change of time from the end of an annual festival to the close of this present world. Both changes etherealise. Both have to put the possessions of the Semitic mind in the ageless sky. The only upward change is a cosmical one. When these things are carefully weighed, it is most evident that the books of the New Testament become devoid of reason, for and in themselves, if the fact of Jesus' transfiguration of Jewish apocalyptic is lost to view. This process then produces a change in the physics of apocalyptic ; nothing more. Jesus becomes the Copernicus of apocalyptic, let us say, to the Ptolemy of Ezekiel. That would be a curious fact for knowledge. It would yield no appreciable help to human beings. Indeed, it could do less for them than the alleged making of their ideas more spiritual as time passed onwards. No one can read the Epistle and be ignorant of its writer's desire to aid his fellows. Therefore something or someone is enthroned over its thought which is greater than any considerations of *cultus* or primary Folk-ideas. That fact is sufficient to dispel the last wisp of the evolutionary myth of apocalyptic.

The Epistle presents no doubt as to whether it is someone or something reigning over its pages. Let the writer complete his picture of Jesus Christ and this fact is amply set out. To do that the opening verses of the Epistle must be joined with the material of chapters i and ii. They are from the same palette as the rest of the picture and of the same canvas. Had

they composed a prologue they would have had colours
and canvas of their own. These they have not. What
is plain is that Jesus is depicted as the Wisdom of God.
The One of the many names receives another ; though
it is not mentioned. He is painted thus for the healing
of the exiled mind. Where in the whole range of
Hebrew literature is brought together the concept of
Wisdom and the exiled mind ? In Baruch iii, 9 to iv,
4 ; and there only. A piece of exquisite research by
the late Dr. Thackeray[1] brought out the peculiar
significance of that passage. He showed that it was a
homily on Wisdom written for the Fast of the 9th of
Ab. Paul had heard this sermon and it has left its
marks on 1 Corinthians i, 18 to ii, 16. He has kept its
outline. In a vivid summary of two names, he turns
the Wisdom which is the Torah into the Wisdom and
the Power which are Jesus Christ. The writer of the
Hebrews dismisses the outline. He keeps its exiles and
their questions. Gives them new intellectual life in the
Epistle. And as well paints with lively strokes the
figure of Jesus Christ as the Wisdom and the Power
of God. Both these writers crown the Ab homily by
leaving the text of Baruch and appropriating that of the
Wisdom of Solomon.[2] That is to say, they borrowed
from the only Sapiential writing which contained its
singular description of the faculties of *Sophia*.
Corinthians etched them in the two names : Hebrews
sketched them in literal order. It was a natural thing
to do ; since the borrowed passage filled in exactly
what the Baruch homily could not, when the two

[1] *The Septuagint and Jewish Worship* (1923), 95 ff.
[2] vii, 22 ff.

F

writers realised how the teaching of the Synagogue was displaced by the revelation of Jesus Christ. The hypothesis of a controversial *florilegium* which could yield the Sapiential material required by Corinthians and Hebrews is an unnatural one. We shall never get things straight in the first century until we learn that the transmutative handling of the Lectionary of the Synagogue by the revelation of Jesus Christ is one of the great creators of New Testament writers and writings. Thus both in that time could be as simple as they ought to be. This realisation makes another modern hypothesis to be equally unwanted. There is no place for the idea that theological speculation, moved on from Judaistic ideas to Græco-Hebraic ones —from the concept of an impersonal Wisdom to the dogma of Jesus Christ as the creative Wisdom of God.[1] A phase of the Hebrew cosmic Idea becoming hellenised into the doctrine of the Person. An Alexandrian achievement before Athens had moulded the Person into the full theory of the Logos. With learning and patience, we of to-day can construct such views. But they of the first century had neither mind nor time for them. Revealer and revelation recreated the men and created their writings. When they used documents for the composition of their messages, these also were subdued to the one commanding and transforming power.

That the writer of the Epistle thus submitted his documents, we have already seen. His usage of them will erase the suspicion from any critical mind that such a view allows him to do with the Lectionary what was

[1] See *supra*, c. i.

denied to the commentators with regard to the Old Testament. The movement from Shebat to Ab is not a restless one : a note of literary caprice. It is ruled by the demands of his exiles' circumstances and the structure of the Epistle. The homily comes to mind because of the Lectionary and contemporary history, and not through recollection of what had been said year by year at the Fast as in the instance of Paul. Both were Jews. Their literary aims were different. The Apostle to the Gentiles was using the Ab homily to turn the flank of Corinthian unwisdom. The writer to the Hebrews was using the whole of the Ab material to woo them to the only Wisdom of God who could come into the world. Both men were doing their work with documentary help at the behest of the revelation of Jesus Christ.

Now when we moderns speak of documents and their use we think of a scholar and his ways with them. This is an idea of which we must rid ourselves when we turn to the New Testament. The writer of our Epistle had his sources written on his brain. Not as a scholar remembers, but as the usages of Folk-religion make a man to know. This is a correct angle of vision we must attain, or the composition of the Epistle will become an exercise of to-day in the writing of a treatise. A passage from the Talmud can give us sight. It also is of supreme importance for the interpretation of the Epistle. In *Ta'anit*[1] we read : " Five calamities happened to our ancestors on the 17th of Tammuz and on the 9th of Ab. On the 17th the tables of Holy Law were broken ; on that day

[1] iv, 6.

continual daily offerings ceased ; then the city of Jerusalem was taken, and Apostomus burned the sacred scrolls and set up an idol in the Temple. On the 9th of Ab it was decreed that our ancestors should not enter the Holy Land ; on that day the first and second Temples were destroyed ; then the city of Bathar was taken, and the site of Jerusalem was ploughed like a field."

Two or three parenthetical remarks must be made on this passage. First it mentions Tammuz as well as Ab. It ought to do so, because Ab is the middle Sabbath of a cycle of six in this period of fasting.[1] There is here then no gentle extension of the dates and material of the Lectionary. Second, it has one anachronous note. The taking of Bathar is not of course a concern of the Epistle. That is a date for the compiling of *Ta'anit*. Third, the name Apostomus is symbolical and not historical. It stands for a desecrator who lived in the Maccabean times.[2] Let the anachronous note be removed ; there is left an harmonious series of topics for Tammuz and Ab which were as gravely momentous for Jewry as they were deeply attaching for converts from Judaism.

From the Epistle's point of view, these calamities were the makers of the exiled mind. Its writer has to meet their effects in Jewish converts. History had placed the assured beliefs of the Folk-mind among the " things that are shaken." Jerusalem ; the Temple ; the Law and the sacrificial system—those subjects,

[1] *E.g.*, Thackeray, 83.
[2] Josephus, *Jewish Wars*, ii, 12, 2 ; *Antiqs.*, xx, 5, 4 ; Ginzberg, *Jewish Encyc.*, ii, 21.

which by long ritual use and veneration had been set
upon timeless foundations—are swept aside by the
storms of Time. It requires little imagination to
follow out the psychological effects of such experiences.
Or to understand that the troubles of the exiled mind
were added to, when these men and women made a new
venture of faith. Their heads would turn back to the
Past. Two great reasons controlled them. It would
be enough for most human beings that the shaking of
immemorial things was alive in their nerves. These
men and women were faced also by an unexplored
land of the mind. Was there any wonder that they
felt the call of the lowland ways ? There can be
none that the Epistle was written to them.

Art and humanity are in all its parts. A twofold
grace which governs the writer's use of the exiles' topics.
He does not hammer them out, as he would if he had
been writing an apology. He hides some within his
tender solicitudes—such as the Temple within the
Tent. Another will slip from his pen in the course of
the powerful statement of a new stability in Jesus
Christ—like the solemn theme " that our ancestors
should not enter into the Holy Land." It is softly
interwoven—first as a citation from Psalm xcv ; then
as a bar or two of austere sound—into the magnificent
comfort of the peerless Apostle's music. There is, of
course, no note of menace in his work. A Semite
would at once be sure of that when he listened to
chapter iii, and be doubly sure of the fact as the themes
of chapter iv began to invade his senses. The Sabbath ;
to Sabbatise ; Rest—what had not these to say to
exiles ? Our writer is here showing the most intimate

side of his art. He knew as they did the inner hurt
those things had for all who cared for Jewry ; and how
they were allied with the topics of Tammuz and Ab.
The Gemara on the passage from *Ta'anit* recalls that
the two Temples were destroyed on " the night of the
Sabbath's close and also on that of the Sabbatical
Year." A little imaginative sympathy on our part will
soon make manifest to us what these things must have
meant to folk just after the overthrow of the second
Temple—that is at the date of the Epistle. The
visible centre of Jewish worship had gone on that night
of nights. Both Jahvistic religion and its day of
worship seemed to be at an end. The very world of
Jahwe stood still in Semitic memory and mind. This
is true even if here is only Folk-tradition and not
history. The sensitive nature of the writer of the
Epistle could appreciate that shock both as man and
artist. He, therefore, is not running off into *haggadah*
which billows and flows as it wills, when he gathers
this and that Old Testament citation or reminiscence
into his narrative. He is giving proof rather of a sort
of musicianship as his Epistle grows. His use of
Psalm xcv is an example. Taking the themes which
worked like pain in the exiled mind, and yet which
held it with the magnetism of " silent voices," he is
lifting both types of inner dismay into the serenity of
the knowledge of the Great High-priest. He is
exquisitely following the curves of the Semitic mind.
Another instance is in his use of the theme of Jerusalem.
That he keeps it until he had brought his exiles home
to Zion is complete evidence for its implicit presence
throughout the Epistle. His exiles have to be made

at home with Revealer and revelation before the
eternal city about an immortal mountain was entered
by them. Moreover he had to be obedient to his
sense of structure.

Let these things be true, the Epistle is still in the
condition of a torn papyrus version. Its fragments are
larger than they were by the discovery of the Shebat
themes. Add these of Tammuz and Ab to them.
We have much yet to recover if the Epistle is to be a
whole document. It will soon be found that Torah
lections of the Fasts will enable us to fill in its thematic
gaps. What are the subjects for which still we have no
source ? To answer this question, we find ourselves
back once more at the beginning of chapter iii. From
that point the subjects of the Epistle are : Moses and
the " House " (iii) ; Joshua (iv) ; Abrahamic covenant
(vii) ; Melchizedek (v and vii) ; Tabernacle (viii and
ix). The exiles' topics, as we have called them,
account already for portions of chapters iii, the wilderness experience ; iv, Sabbath and Rest ; viii, Temple ;
ix and x, Sacrifice. The subject of Melchizedek
demands special treatment ; since it is totally apart
from this portion of the Lectionary of the Synagogue.
And the Maccabean factor belongs to the joint problems
of structure and subject with an almost identical
independence of that treasure-house of documents.
When from the above summary of subjects that of
Melchizedek is withdrawn, we are left with four
primary ones whose sources must be found.

Those subjects come at once to the eye from the
Torah lections of Ab and Tammuz. For instance,
Exodus xxxiii and Numbers xxvii and Deuteronomy iii

yield the Joshua theme.   Deuteronomy iv and Exodus xxxii that of the Abrahamic covenant.   Exodus xxxiii and Numbers xxxi offer the subjects of the Tabernacle and the Levitical priesthood.   It has to be remembered that these Torah readings had the chance of doubly impressing themselves on the writer's sensitive mind. Ab and Tammuz either have the same readings or they repeat the same subjects in different readings.   There can be no doubt of their effectiveness of suggestion, both for the matter and the structure of the Epistle. The former demonstrates itself ;   the latter has to be demonstrated.   Hebrews xii, 29 makes the puzzling assertion :   " for our God is a consuming fire."   The writer is, of course, closing his Epistle[1] with a citation from the dominating Torah lection of Ab, that is Deuteronomy iv.   From his first verse to his last he is working with the freedom of a musician within the strictures of form.

It will be noticed that the Fasts have accounted for three out of the four primary subjects.   What of Moses and the " House " ?   We have found that when our writer seeks Lectionary material for his Epistle which is outside the usage of Ab and Tammuz, then either one of the two creative literary factors of his work will choose for him the portion of the Lectionary he should employ.   The Maccabean factor singled out Shebat.   The Ab factor sends him to Siwan.   Its homily is embodied in Baruch.   The first chapter of that writing clusters together the feelings and reasons

[1] The style and vocabulary of chapter xiii mark it as not belonging to Hebrews.   It is most probably a portion of a lost Pauline epistle.   See also *infra* in chapter vi.

for the Fast after the fall of the first temple, and centres them about a traditional date in Siwan. There is no evidence that it could be a festal date, even though it were argued that the Syriac version seems to have considered it to be one.[1] Our writer is doing here as he did with 1 Maccabees. That, after all, is our chief concern. Then the Moses and " House " subject comes from Numbers xii which is a part of the Torah lection for the third Sabbath in Siwan. Further its prophetical lection, Zechariah iii, yields the important subject of Joshua. Once more the other side of the evidence naturally appears for the choice of Lectionary material by the writer to the Hebrews— it must have the same topical reference as that of his major source. If we turn back to the Torah portions for Siwan, we find other agreements. Numbers viii and ix have the subject of Tabernacle and Levites. Numbers xiv the Joshua and Wilderness themes. These again are duplicated in the prophetical reading for the fourth of Siwan, that is in Joshua ii. That this lection is structurally necessary to the Epistle can be detected in the delicate and natural fashion which such considerations have a right to demand. We know now why Rahab comes into chapter xii. She is there because one of the writer's Lectionary sources has been touched by the golden rod of the revelation of Jesus Christ. That is a subject we shall look into again. For the present we may note the delicacy and naturalness of his workmanship, when we follow from source to text.

---

[1] It reads " 10th of Nisan " for Siwan. Thackeray, 93, wants to banish the month from the text. Others want to shift it from verse 8 to verse 14. That could make it a festal date, which it is not. Its use by Hebrews proves that the month was Siwan.

And its indelicacy and unnaturalness when we hypothesise that he was a Christological speculative writing to Ephesus ; and then have to enlarge our hypothesis thus : " Rahab would not naturally be cited as a model of faith except in a church where that virtue had been ascribed to her in a work regarded as a religious classic."[1] Thus he is denied simplicity of commerce between sources and Epistle, and the woman one natural touch of a wand which could transport her from Joshua ii into Hebrews xi. Such a detail is due as much to beauty of thought as delicacy of artistry.

This rare combination of qualities will surely have shown itself in the handling of the theme of Moses and the " House." At least we shall be doing what is right to give more attention to that subject ; since the greater themes of Apostle and High-priest are woven together with it. To this end the views of the Dutch scholar, which have before supplied us with much food for thought, will be again interrogated. For him the theme of Moses and the " House " comes from a controversial *florilegium* wherein it has played an anti-Judaic part against the conception of the Old " House " which is the Temple. Its base is a *testimonium* in that document, Numbers xii, 7 ; and Justin's[2] evidence on this point is claimed as able to warrant the conclusion that the whole subject belongs to *anti-Judaica* which pre-dated the Epistle[3]. On Cyprian's[4] and Lactantius'[5] evidence it is claimed that Jesus as the High-Priest

---

[1] Streeter, 194.
[2] *Trypho*, xlvi ; lvi ; cxxx.
[3] Plooij, 40 ff.
[4] *Testimonia*, i, xvi.
[5] *Div. Inst.*, iv, 14.

springs from the same source, and in particular
1 Samuel ii, 35 f. What of the title Apostle ? Plooij
can cite only Justin's first *Apology*.[1] There Jesus
Christ is called Son of God and Apostle ; and one of the
names for the *Logos* is said to be Apostle. His
Trypho[2] offers no help ; since it contents itself with
calling prophets ἀπόστολοι. An appeal to the
Cyprianic *Testimonia*,[3] where Jesus is given the name
of Angel, inspires him to efforts to save the situation.
Under this name is grouped the citation Exodus xxiii,
20 ff. Because the bishop of Carthage had or edited a
text of that passage which did not yield the name,
Plooij goes away to the Samaritan Targum on Exodus
xxiii and finds it there. He concludes from this that
either the Epistle, or the anti-Judaic text used by its
writer, had avoided calling Jesus by the name of
Angel and had substituted its Targum alternative,
Apostle.

Both sources, structure and thought of the Epistle
deny the validity of these conclusions. There is not
one anti-Judaic note in the document. It draws
its literary substance from the Lectionary of the
Synagogue not to controvert but to transmute Jewish
material, not to antagonise but to win Jews. It goes
direct to the primary source, and turns its spoil into gold
for the mind by the revelation of Jesus Christ. It did
not go to a secondary source ; first having to purge it
from anti-Judaism, and then changing it into winsome
values. The writer of the Epistle could not jeopardise

---

[1] 12 and 63.
[2] lxxv.
[3] ii, v.

this lovely crystallisation of source and thought—an achievement of native genius and not of æsthetic theory —by such roundabout methods. The certainty that this man was drawing directly on the Lectionary reasserts the view that Justin, for example, is in turn drawing upon the Epistle ; and that the fourth-century Latin writers are using an anti-Judaic authority which also has taken some of its material from the Epistle and placed it in a controversial framework.

The most interesting problem of the name Apostle remains. No help is forthcoming from the Septuagint. 1 Kings xiv, 6 is the only example of its use. Of the ancient Greek translators Aquila has the same rendering in that passage. Whilst Symmachus uses the word in Isaiah xviii, 2. The hypothesis that our writer would need a Concordance or have erudite recourse to an ancient and individual translation of the Old Testament has not been nor is likely to be advanced. When the Dutch scholar turned to the Samaritan Targum he made, however, something like the same erudite *détour*. Had he gone on to accumulate more Samaritan evidence for the name Apostle, as applied to Moses, he would have prevented our author from seeming treason to his natural art and himself from building an unwanted textual theory. This evidence can be enlarged, for example, by the help of the early Arabo-Samaritan commentary upon the most ancient extant writing in the Samaritan language, *The Secrets of Moses*.[1] This commentary to a " Life of Moses," which in reality is but a portion of the Semitic Folk-saga of the " Sons of the Man," contains much lore which was known at

[1] Gaster, *The Asatir* (1927).

least as far back as the first century, and especially the tales about Moses.[1] The Samaritans then have kept clear memory of more of this Folk-lore than the Jews. *The Secrets of Moses* and its commentary are nearer the mind of the Semites than the Pentateuch. In the latter the name Apostle (*i.e.*, Messenger or Revealer) is given no less than ten times to Moses.[2] Of these, two will be chosen out because of their contextual significance. The first occurs in an account of his birth, some of whose remarkable details have found their way into the New Testament.[3] The second gives Moses that name when mentioning two other " Sons of the Man "—one of them is Joshua—and after citing Joshua xxiv, 17. This is the *logion* which, with a small group like itself, becomes the basis of *anti-Judaica* current in the second and subsequent centuries.[4] Our title takes us back to the hebraic source of such controversial instruments rather than to their Christian embodiments. A glance over our evidence will bring out the fact that the author of the Hebrews was making no recondite reference when he used the name Apostle or Revealer for Moses and Jesus Christ. He had call neither to go to a Samaritan source nor to a supposed Hebrew Targum for the name. It is evident

[1] See my book for proofs.

[2] Five other instances occur in the story of Moses' death from a Samaritan Chronicle edited by Gaster, 302 ff.

[3] *Asatir*, viii, 31 ; Samaritan Comm : viii (163).

[4] *A*. x, 45 ; S.C., x (134). The other Apostle references are: *A*. viii, 23, S.C., viii (96) ; *A*. ix, 18, S.C. viii (109) ; *A*. x, 40, S.C., x (133) ; *A*. xi, 3, S.C., xi (144) ; *A*. xi, 25, S.C., xi (149) ; *A*. xii, 39, S.C., viii (164) ; and a second time at this place. My findings concerning the basis of *anti-Judaica* will be developed elsewhere. Gaster's views, 88 ff. are important.

that it was a well-recognised factor in the Folk-saga of Moses : a principal component, that is to say, of Jewish apocalyptic. In that area the writer was at work. Thence the name had come into the Epistle ; and by a touch from His revelation had become an eminent name for Jesus Christ. With Him it had entered into its true estate.

We have laid bare the sources and structure of the Epistle so that only the Melchizedek feature and the Maccabean factor remain unexamined. To the point we have reached, we find it governed by flawless and simple interactions. The Semitic Folk-mind and the revelation of Jesus ; the exile and the disciple—these interact in a mind of singular directness and sensitiveness, and within a clearly marked area of Festival literature and time. Thus what have been called topics of the exiled mind and Lectionary subjects fuse in a message of healing to the bewildered. They were bound to do so. The writer has the same ease and naturalness of access to Lectionary and Revealer. Nothing could be farther from his genius than an argument of an Alexandrian character against speculative Judaism ;[1] unless it be the claim that his purpose was to elaborate an argument on sacrifice to

---

[1] *E.g.*, Häring, *Zur Frage nach dem Zweck und Leserkreis des Hebräerbriefs* (*Studien und Kritiken*, 1891) 594 ff. Against this view may be cited the Ab homily, iii, 22, with its decision against any other than Hebrew thought—see Ewald, *Geschichte des Volkes Israel* iii, 292 ; Kneucker, *Das Buch Baruch* (1879), 292 ; Kalt, *Das Buch Baruch* (1932), 17. Knabenbauer, *Commentarius in Danielem Prophetam, Lamentationes et Baruch* (1891) maintains the conventional Patristic views on all the problems of Baruch. That is typical of those students of this extra-canonical work who are unaware of its problems.

meet its problems for normative Judaism of the first century.[1] Judge his statement on the latter subject by those interactions, and you will find the Epistle open to you. The terms of his statement must be carefully kept in balance or their work will be missed. For him the Apostle or Revealer precedes the High-priest. If it can be said with any accuracy that there is approach to argument in the Epistle, the term must be applied to what he says about the Revealer rather than about sacrifice. We have but to read from chapter iii onwards to be assured of the truth of that judgment. When we turn from its letter to follow the exquisite interplay of Semite and Christian in the document, then we realise the utter grace of its craftsmanship is due to a grasp of Semitic things which is beautiful sympathy, and a response to the revelation of Jesus Christ which is rare discipleship.

Doctrine is not written by such a man. He is the realiser of the fascination of the lowland ways in the time of the great Fasts and the wooer of men upwards, because of the delightful lucidity of his understanding of and consecration to the Revealer ; upon whom the turning of no festal calendar can cast a shadow.

[1] Purdy, 263 ff.

CHAPTER V

THE UNIQUE KING OF PEACE AND THE POWERS OF HIS REVELATION

THE distance between Philo and the Epistle is nowhere seen with such clarity as when a comparison is attempted of what they did with Melchizedek. The Alexandrian tries to turn Genesis xiv into myth after the style of his master Plato. He produces myth with Platonic savour but not with Platonic elegance and mastery. In one place,[1] Melchizedek the king of righteousness is the royal soul of man under the control of right reason. When he offers bread to Abraham, Melchizedek the priest is the *Logos* informing that soul with high and majestic thoughts. The awkward versatility of the priest-king is at least one sign that myths were not as naturally turned in Alexandria as in Athens. In another place,[2] Melchizedek is the creative *Logos* or Word, whose father was Jahwe and mother *Sophia* or Wisdom. His priestly robes are the beauty of the world. If he took off his mitre, his powers and sanctions would go from him. Let his robes be rent, both the actuality and

[1] *Legum alleg.* iii, 79 ff.
[2] *De Fuga,* 108 ff.

beauty of the cosmic scheme of things would be shattered. Could Plato have made this myth, its surface would have been like silk where there was any question of the union of ideas with mixed nationality. He also would have shrunk from the naïve nature of Philo's art.

We can compare Philo and Plato. We cannot compare Philo with the Epistle. Things must touch where comparison can be made. To establish connexions between the Alexandrian and Hebrews something of this sort would have to go on in chapters v and vii. The writer would have become a literary anatomist whose portrait Lewis Carroll ought to have drawn. He must strip the philonic Melchizedek of all that was hellenic to make him an hebraic figure. To get to the bare features of the tradition of the priest-king, he would remove their filmy coverings from them. Plato, *Logos* philosophy and *Sophia* speculation of late Hebrew thought and Philo's own ways in interpretation—these close coverings would have to come away before he got to the tradition. When they had gone, he would still have to exorcise what of them had passed into its substance. If success attended his work concerning those lively and subtle invaders, he would have the tradition in its original hebraic form. Our author does not think and work in that ambulant way. What he says of Melchizedek, he could take from Genesis xiv or from a well-known tradition. The simplicity of fusion between art and material in this man makes it certain that if he had used Alexandrian thought he would have done so in a plain manner. We should have known the fact. Plato would be there, though his

G

speech was tinged with Hebrew. He is not in the
Epistle. Philo is also an absentee from its text.
Further, the writer nowhere shows that his art might
have been exercised in Alice's world of the Looking-
Glass. The bare features of the Melchizedek tradition,
however, are there. They also are in contexts which
preclude platonic connivance and constituents.

The problem whether it is exact or inexact to assert
that Philo is an influence in the Epistle has now been
raised in an acute form. Context and structure can
best give an answer. They are united by the artless art
of the writer so that Alexandria must be or not be their
significant tie. If Græco-Egyptian influence be
removed, then according to the view of its advocates
the whole document should fall apart. We ought to
be left with some Hebrew pieces and some Christian
pieces that lack the one quality which can make them
literature. This view can be tested on two Scots
writers. Kennedy, whose judgment as a rule was in
careful control, has said that he cannot help finding the
influence of Philo in the Epistle and especially in its
statement of the priesthood of Jesus Christ.[1] It must
be submitted that this opinion owes more to a late
doctrine of the hellenisation of the Bible than to the
objective study of the Epistle's text. Moffatt,[2] who is
the commentators' gifted heir, touches this great
subject and at once begins to weave about it philonic
webs. There is no trouble to find illustrations, for
instance, in his treatment of chapter v. This high-
priest " who can bear gently with the ignorant and the

[1] Kennedy, *Philo's Contribution to Religion* (1919), 170.
[2] Moffatt, 61 ff.

erring " presents a problem in vocabulary. The verb is marked down as philonic[1] and from an ethical philosopher's list of words. Both claims as to the literal use of the word may be true. That the word should be thus exclusively designated points to the commentator's intellectual predisposition and not to a demand of the text upon which he is at work. A better analogue could have been found in Plutarch.[2] This engaging writer is not looked at. Though there is much more in his attitude to men and problems than in Philo's which might inspire fruitful comparisons with the writer of the Epistle. The commentator moves on to the next verse where the high-priest is said to be bound to make offering for his own and the people's sins. It is not enough to see in the word what every Jewish reader would perceive in them, that is a commonplace of Levitical practice : the commentator must draw attention to the fact that Philo[3] recognises this two-fold form of sacrifice. Of course he would when glossing the life of Moses in his own manner. What the Alexandrian did with the Pentateuch is after all no concern of the Epistle to the Hebrews. It ought not to be a concern of his commentator. He too has his responsibility towards his readers who will be led another step on the way of the final philonisation of a New Testament writing. From the third we may go on to the ninth verse, where it is said of Jesus Christ that " he became unto all them that

---

[1] Moffatt *ad loc.*

[2] *Consolatio ad Apollonium, Moralia*, ii, 102D. Josephus, *Antiqs.*, xii, 32, is another important parallel.

[3] *De Vita Mosis*, ii, 7.

obey the αἴτιος of eternal salvation." For that
Greek word Moffatt turned, as do other recent commentators, to Philo[1] again. Here he admits the inade-
quacy of the parallel. The Alexandrian is referring, he
says, to Abraham and Genesis xxiii, 6, and not to
Melchizedek. That is textually accurate. It is not,
however, exegetically appropriate. A fold or two more
of philonic mist is put about the text of the Epistle.
Some momentum has been added to the tendency to
turn the document into theological typology. The
ordinary intelligent mortal, who is the person that
matters in the end, stumbles forward on a tableland
unto which Jesus Christ is neither sun nor moon. The
mist will not allow Him to be one or the other. There
is no call to seek recondite parallel or source for our
writer. This particular word comes from a source
which, as we shall see, was well used by him. It is a
Maccabean word, both in the singular and in the
plural.[2] One other illustration, and this time one
which links together chapters v, vi and vii. In the
tenth verse of chapter v, the twentieth verse of chapter
vi, and several verses of chapter vii, he makes use of
Psalm cx, 4: " Thou art a priest for ever after the
order of Melchizedek." Moffatt's exegesis has led
him to assert that Hebrews has found the idea of the
permanency of the Melchizedekian priesthood by
explaining the Psalm from Genesis xiv. To this the
writer added " the Alexandrian principle that the very
silence of scripture is charged with meaning." What
was said by adding Genesis to Psalm and what was not

---

[1] *De Abrahamo*, 45.
[2] 2 Macc. iv, 47, xiii, 4 ; 4 Macc. i, 11.

said in the Old Testament were the interpretative leads to the timeless character of that priesthood. This exegesis from silence is justified by several illustrations from Philo.[1] The implication surely is that our writer will follow his exemplary exegete. It will be shown later that at no point is the Epistle farther from Philonism than where it makes use of Psalm cx.

A review of these claims and the running comments upon them manifests that as concerns the philonic seed and shape of the idea of priesthood ; or the philonic vocabulary of the chapters in which it is contained ; or the putting of philonic parallels to those chapters ; or the claim that the exegetical methods of the writer were learnt from Philo—these all can be removed from the Epistle and it will remain intact. There is no injury to its parts, either by way of dislocation or disruption. Indeed, it will be shown that only as the Epistle is rid of Alexandria can it speak its authentic message.

A proper preparation for the fresh study of context and structure will be found in readjusting the perspective of recent interpretation of Jesus the High-Priest. The settled opinion that Hebrews is an essay in Christological theory is the cause of error in our angle of vision. When the Epistle lays its foundation for the concept, it keeps together two great names for Jesus— " the Apostle and High-Priest of our confession," or as we have had to read the sentence, " the Revealer and High-Priest of our confession." When technical Christology takes possession of the document, the

---

[1] The writer of the Epistle is nowhere the forerunner of Origen.

name Apostle is lost to view. A doctrine of Sonship
informs the name Son ; and it companions the name
High-Priest, which also is more of a doctrine than a
name. Son becomes a supreme divine rôle : High-
Priest becomes an allegory of that Son's chief attribute
by the help of Melchizedek. The Epistle is said to
look at the historical Jesus through those two eyes. His
work is defined by what they see, and not by what He
did and was. The Revealer and His revelation are not
seen. There can be no wonder that the name Apostle
or Revealer is erased from the thought of the Epistle.
Christology has not yet learnt its use.

What is primary for the Epistle ought to be primary
for us. Exegetes may not erase, evacuate, or exclude
such a factor. To do any of these is to misconceive
both Moses and Jesus Christ—and therefore the
document in which they come. Evidence is already
before us which demonstrates that in the Semitic Folk-
saga of Moses this was his unique name. To that,
other and even more important evidence can be added.
For example, ancient Samaritan tradition[1] denominates
the Sinai incident of the giving of the Law, Exodus xix,
as the day of revelation and calls Moses by the name of
Apostle or Revealer. Further, it associates the ideas
and names of revelation and Revealer with Moses'
declaration of what we know as the " Song of Moses,"
Deuteronomy xxxii. The age of the tradition is not
affected by the fact that these things have become
features in mediæval Samaritan eschatology. Early
Hebrew evidence shows, for instance, that Semitic

---

[1] *Yom al-Din*, xxvi, xcvi—see Gaster, *Samaritan Eschatology*
(1932), i, 119, 124 ff.

apocalyptic has in Deuteronomy xxxii a principal
literary inspiration. Psalm lxxxi is the proper psalm
for New Year's Day. Its verses thirteen and
sixteen are citations of the " Song."[1] Whilst 1
Samuel ii, 2, which is its distinctive prophetical
lection,[2] again cites that document. Another festival
offers the same sort of evidence. One of the prophetical
lections for Ab was Hosea xiv. Its ninth verse is from
Deuteronomy xxxii. That verse has its exact analogue
in the opening of the Baruch homily of the Fast[3]. Such
illustrations could be multiplied many times over.
They do not use the name Revealer for Moses. They
cite his revelation. The name, therefore, is implied
in many parts of the Old Testament. It is a possession
also of the Semitic mind, seeing that Deuteronomy
xxxii belongs to the core of Jewish apocalyptic. No
one can fail to grasp the significance for the Epistle
of certain of these illustrations. The traditional
association of the name with a Torah lesson which has
profoundly influenced its structure ; the same connexions with the most ancient ritual canticle ; the place
of that " Song " in the text of the Epistle and its
infolded relationships with Ab—these are some of the
reasons why the writer of the Epistle will give first
place in its thought to the idea and name of Apostle or
Revealer. Moses for the Semite is not Moses without
that function and name. To place him over against
Jesus Christ without them would reduce him to the

---

[1] Gaster, 80 ; see *Rosh Hashanah*, 30b for place of the Psalm
in the liturgy.
[2] Thackeray, *Song of Hannah and the Jewish New Year's Day,
Journal of Theological Studies*, xvi, 177 ff.
[3] Gaster, 79 ; Thackeray, *Septuagint*, 96.

condition of a lay figure. To deprive Jesus Christ of them robs Him of historicity and His power to trans-figure the prime motions of the Folk-mind as they insensibly lead men home to His revelation. When these grave matters are looked at from the Epistle's standpoint, we ought to see that without them as positive and ruling possessions it is a document which has no meaning. The fundamental brainwork of the writer, in its evangel and structure, is set at nought. In his first chapter he has put the Son as one of a list of names for Jesus Christ. He nowhere makes it a commanding theological factor. Therefore, it is used as a name in chapter v. It occurs with the same context as in chapter i. The revelation of Jesus Christ had turned an item of apocalyptic into a name for the historic Revealer. The name recurs in chapter v with the same transmuted significance. A singular Semitic name for Moses has become the most unique title in religion because it is now borne by Jesus Christ. A function which was ascribed by the devout Folk-mind to the Lawgiver has become the most natural and unparalleled fact in the history of religion because it is the very *raison d'être* of Jesus Christ. That fact and function reign over the Epistle from its beginning to its end. Their recognition is the best of all guides for the understanding of its contexts and structure.

In chapter i the name Son is attested by Psalm ii, 7. Both name and source are repeated in chapter v, and are followed by another which yields the name Priest—that is Psalm cx, 4. There is large necessity that we should grasp this use of the new attestator. The elementary reason for its presence is the name. In practice our writer treats it as if it had yielded two names, Priest and High-Priest. That is not wayward usage on his part, but natural nominal growth. He has to meet two factors of the composition of his Epistle : the Lectionary factor and the Maccabean factor. Each requiring a name for Jesus, if His revelation touches them into new values. The writer binds them together in the *testimonium*, Psalm cx, 4. This transaction is quite clear as to the Lectionary. What have the Maccabees to do with the matter ? Some gleams of the far-reaching influence of the Maccabean factor in the Epistle have already been shown. Here are others. The first of these begins to light up the reason why Psalms ii and cx were chosen by the writer, and the second commences to show why any reference should be made to Melchizedek.

Merx,[1] for example, believed Psalm ii to be a Maccabean song. It is used as such in Hebrews. Moreover, there are many new reasons for upholding this view, which will be given in due course. From Bickell[2] to Gowan,[3] the critics have granted the Maccabean character of Psalm cx. Though Briggs[4] has endeavoured to prove that the phrase " after the order of Melchizedek " is a gloss on the original text, it is plain that for the Epistle those words were an important part of the Psalm. They form one half of the reason for its choice. Again fresh reasons other than this textual one, as for Psalm ii, will be offered.

[1] *Festschrift zu Ehren von David Chwolson* (1899), 198 ff.
[2] Cited, *e.g.*, by Briggs *ad loc.*
[3] *The Psalms* (1930), 368.
[4] *The Book of the Psalms* (1907), ii, 374.

From the structural point of view, it should be noted what a place has been given to the two Psalms in the text of Hebrews. In it Psalm cx, 4, appears at fourteen different places. That is evidence for the bulk of the Maccabean factor in its writer's mind.

The inclination will be to put into that sentence Melchizedekian instead of Maccabean factor. Though natural it would be a wrong one. A suggestion why can be given at this point without anticipating what will be said in the last section of this study. In Florence is preserved an ancient manuscript containing the Peshitto version of the Old Testament. After the text of 4 Maccabees follows a Syriac rendering of Josephus' *Jewish Wars*, Book vi.[1] It bears the title, 5 *Maccabees*. In all other respects it is like the original Greek. Most of its text is taken up with the story of the overthrow of Jerusalem by Titus. The terrible sufferings and remarkable heroism of the Jews ; and the shameful surrender of the Temple treasures— compose an epic. The book is timed in the seasons of Ab and Tammuz. To its closing episode is attached the fact of Vespasian's destruction of the city ; and blended with it comes the tradition of Melchizedek,[2] a Canaanite chieftain, the original founder of Jerusalem. He is said to have given the city that name. From these things arise the suggestion that Melchizedek finds his place in the Epistle through its Maccabean factor. When, in the first century and after the fall of the second Temple, the Maccabees were thought

---

[1] Ceriani, *Translatio Syra Pescitto Vetus Testamenti*, (1876) ii, 660 ff.
[2] *Bell. Jud.*, vi, x, 438.

about, then the tradition of the founder of the city and the builder of the original Temple was brought vividly to the Folk-memory. The Syriac title of the narrative of those facts preserves the ancient and valuable tradition. There is no reason at all for making Josephus a source for the Epistle. It is altogether free of the Jewish historian. Josephus, in the shape of a Syriac version of a book from his *Jewish Wars*, is an epitome of contemporaneous tradition. The writer of the Epistle finds his union with the historian, not so much in what he records as in the Palestinian popular name which was given to the body of tradition he has narrated. This included the story of the first founder of city[1] and temple. It is plain that the exiled mind, in a time of the break-up of its native religious world, will go back to him. It is also plain that the writer, with his lively Maccabean interests, will introduce the material of the priest-king's tradition because of the greater and nearer factor.

If the material of the tradition of Melchizedek came into the Epistle in the above manner, how came the person? Just as Moses came into the document. That is by way of the Lectionary of the Synagogue. Its traditional inspiration is balanced by its religious inspiration. Moses came along the natural path of the Torah lections of Shebat and Ab. Melchizedek comes into the Epistle along a nearby pathway. We have already found the list of names in the Isaian lection for Shebat at work in Hebrews. Isaiah ix, 6, contains much more which has not yet been noticed.

---

[1] *Cf.* Theophilus of Antioch, *Ad Autolycum*, ii, 31.

First of all, the name King of Peace. The unusual
Greek version of this passage preserves that name in
this form, ἄρχων εἰρήνης. That noun of course means
King. Æschylus,[1] for instance, thus uses the word.
But is the Epistle influenced by this Shebat lection in
chapter vii as it was in chapter ii ? After the name is
used, the writer proceeds to say that its holder was
" without father, mother, ancestry, beginning of days
and end of life." Put the name back into its Isaian
context, and the source of such a statement is found.
Its King of Peace is the nation's son, the manifestation
of Jahwe : himself known as the Father of all the ages
and God. Therefore our writer has simply para-
phrased the whole lection, besides using one of the
names literally and another allusively.[2] He is not
indulging in fantasy of interpretation, as we have been
told that he was.[3] He is faithful to his source. All
this, it will be perceived, is matter which can have
nothing to do with Genesis xiv. It offers most
adequate reasons why we should claim that
Melchizedek's pathway into the Epistle was Isaiah ix, 6
and 7.

The potency of this lection is not exhausted.
Hebrews vii gives the priest-king another name, King
of Righteousness. It is not enough to say of this one
that the writer is merely interpreting Melchizedek ; nor
to retort that it at least is not in the Isaian list. The
first opinion sees the name only in a contextual sentence
or two and ignores its influence on much of the latter

---

[1] *Pers.*, 74.
[2] See *supra*, c. iii ff.
[3] *Cf.* Moffatt, 91.

half of the Epistle. The second opinion does not realise that the conceptions which created the name are in Isaiah ix, and that these compose the sole reasons why this passage exists. Before the task is undertaken of bringing out these things, we should note that the foundation of Hebrews vii, 2 and 3, is made up of three names. Two of them have been traced to the Shebat lection. The third also is from the same source. It is the name Son. As they stand, the name and its accompanying phrase look as if there were dual reference in them; that is back to Isaiah ix and on to Jesus Christ. Their common rendering is, "made like unto the Son of God." Thus the statement is treated as an item in the Christology of the Epistle. Its author is said to be drawing a portrait of Melchizedek. Not in a real sense, but in such a manner as to make him suggest Jesus Christ.[1] The verb in the phrase should be translated "resembling." Just as must be done with the word in the *Epistle of Jeremy*, 70. Recognising that what goes before this phrase in Hebrews comes from Isaiah ix, it seems more likely that it too is a reflection of the Shebat lesson. Therefore its significance for the writer will not be Christologic but Elohistic. That is to say, Melchizedek bears the divine signs of autogenesis which are in that lesson, "resembling (*i.e.*, like to) a son of El"; for such is the divine name at this place in the prophet. Then the parallel to the phrase is Daniel iii, 25, "like to a son of the gods"[2]—a verse

---

[1] *E.g.*, Dods and Davidson, *Expositor's Greek Testament*, iv, 308.

[2] Moffatt, 97, remarks of this Danielic word which is used in Hebrews vii, 15 "linguistically has the same sense" as the word used in Hebrews vii, 3.

which also used to be considered a Christological one. The recognition of these names as belonging to Melchizedek and their derivation from one of the few sources drawn upon by the writer of the Epistle, yields another instance of the type of workmanship which is his own. The sense of the Epistle is thereby also enriched. We have now to turn to the remaining name, King of Righteousness. A full examination of which will throw light on very much of importance in the Epistle and on everything in the lesson from the Lectionary.

First, the source ; and then, our writer's use of the source. The Son of El with the many names, which are divine attributes or powers,[1] will maintain his kingdom by equity and righteousness and in peace for ever. These powers he will exercise from the Davidic throne in Jerusalem. The details do not any longer compose for us a piece of messianism : the theological putting of the geographical Jerusalem in the sunrise of some far-off end of things or in the cleansed sky. Robertson Smith[2] on the side of anthropology, and the Danish scholar Pedersen[3] on the sides of anthropology and philology, have enabled us to grasp their actual significance. The terms in the lection which for us have taken on the hard meanings of juridical and regal practice—and so the formal ones of theology— now have the sensitive meanings of the primitive biology of society whence they came. Walls and

---

[1] Cf. Hebrew Enoch, xlviii, C9.

[2] Cf. Cook, Cambridge Ancient History (1924), ii, 398 ; Johnson, The Rôle of the King in the Jerusalem Cultus (Hooke, The Labyrinth, 1935), 76.

[3] Israel, Its Life and Culture (1926).

towers go : the judicial sentences and sceptred decrees pass away. The terms, King, equity, righteousness and established peace, which appear to mean little or nothing else but those things, now give expression to the primary things of Semitic sociology. By the help of a descriptive which Pedersen uses, we can go directly to the heart of the subject ; and so avoid the technicalities of Semitic anthropology and philology. He has made familiar the term, psychic community. It describes the fundamental pattern of Semitic social life. It also sums up all that those terms can mean which we turn into implements of legal and regal activity in an eschatological world.

This term, psychic community, has nothing to do with spiritualism or of being fey as certain Celts are said to be. It defines kinship : the actual connexions of the begetter and the begotten. The relationship of father and son ; king and son ; Jahwe and Son. In its light these three are not the separate though primary data of Semitic society : the social, constitutional and religious circles whose centres are always different but whose circumferences may touch. They are struck from one centre. Concentric, not as a mathematician describes circles but as Life strikes them. Whether you look at them from the lowliest Semite and his son up to Jahwe and his Son, or from the Jahwe group to that family group, the same picture of vital interoperations presents itself. The lowly has as much need of the high as the high of the lowly, if the community is to be kept alive. It is kept alive not in the sense of its continuance but as concerns its reciprocities unto life. These maintain it whole. Bread and the Order of civilisation preserve a modern State. Veneration and Jahvistic response upheld this Semitic State. The condition of sonship in it was ever and everywhere the channel of both. Its throne on which was the Son was a physical fount and not as with us a moral symbol. That is not hyperbole. Here we come upon the great cosmical feature of its cult scheme. The throne is on the Centre of the earth, and is set over the fountain of waters which fertilises man and Nature.[1] Rain is the obverse of the idea of life to the psychic community. Judgment is its reverse ; seeing that as it fell or was held back so the sentence of the favour or disfavour of Jahwe was manifested towards its members. They who occupied the throne were of most ancient lineage ; for they were " Sons of the Man."[2] They were not less royal because their sceptre was often used as a rain-maker's rod.[3] The flow of life from the throne was regulated as much by him who sat thereon as by the worshipping spirit of its most modest subject. Another contrast with our own national society will bring out the foundation feature of

[1] Wensinck, *Verhandelingen der Koninklijke Akademie Wentenschappen te Amsterdam*, Af. Letterkunde, N.R., xvii, 1, (1916), 54 ff. My book shows that when first century writers are dealing with this subject they go back to the rain-rite which lies behind its usage in the greater festivals of the Jewish Year. Thus there is no reason why the connexions between rain and the psychic community should be limited to the Feast of Tabernacles as Johnson, 85 ff.

[2] When the writer of the Epistle gives Jesus the names of Man and Son of the Man in chapter ii he is linking Him with what underlies chapter vii.

[3] *Cf. Asatir*, ix, 22, " The rod of Adam and his robes were given to Moses " ; and Exodus iv, 20, " rod of El," or perhaps " rod of the gods " ; see also *Asatir*, iii, 25, where the Samaritan can bear both renderings.

this Semitic society. The King reigns by the grace of God and his people's affection, those loftier sanctions of the Order of civilisation. The King of Peace or Righteousness reigned by life from Jahwe and his people's responsive faith as they venerated him as Jahwe's surrogate. Such is a picture of the psychic community. We can see it at work if we will turn to the true meanings of terms like peace, righteousness and covenant.

If now we put those first two terms back into the Shebat lection, we shall have them in those conditions where a lexicon can properly deal with them. It will be noticed that the community rules the passage and its context. The Son is the nation's child. Peace and righteousness are the results of his being the King of Peace. His other names mount up to that one. He is not the Perfect Pacifist, but the king who bears divine names and powers. He is derivatively their Son.[1] It is these which knit together him and his kingdom. Their increase will mean the lasting establishment of the community. How then do they grow ?

The Hebrew word for Peace and its first allies harmonise in their meanings. Any excellent lexicon shows that as a matter of course. What this estimable volume does not point out is that these meanings fit into the concentrics of the Semitic community, according to our picture of them, as does life in an

---

[1] *Cf. e.g., Hebrew Enoch* xiii, 1, where Rabbi Ishmael was crowned with the letters of the names by which the cosmos was created. Later he sees these names shining on the Throne of Glory, xli, 1 ff.

H

organism. Each has its being by the something within. An interrogation of the Hebrew word *Shalom*[1] evokes that it is a quintessence of Semitic sociology. Man ; family ; social community and that totality in connexion with the divine are in the word. Each of those four phases is represented by it in active and right condition. That is as sound, complete and balanced. Just as a man is a man whose powers are in a state of equipoise, that fine harmony of well-being. So is a family or a community of men and families only those when its members are one of another, that more splendid harmony of interactive well-being. These are what is meant by Peace. Three illustrations of this achievement will be enough to demonstrate these definitions. First one that this Peace implies a psychic community. When David blessed Solomon before the people,[2] he petitioned Jahwe to maintain for ever veneration in the being of the worshipping society and to give his son a being at Peace by the keeping of the commandments and statutes and the doing of reverence to Jahwe. The basic spiritual reciprocities which compose the community could not be more profoundly and simply told. Our two other illustrations equally help us to understand its nature.

When Moses was on the throne of another mountain and Centre than the one in Jerusalem, Jethro visited him and said,[3] " I thy father-in-law am come unto thee, and thy wife and her two sons with her." And Moses

---

[1] See especially Pedersen, 263 ff.

[2] 1 Chron. xxix, 18 ff. ; see Pedersen 336 ff. Also *cf.* 1 Kings xv, 14 f. ; 2 Kings xx, 3, and Deuteronomy iv, 29 ff., vi, 4 ff.

[3] Exodus xviii, 6 ff.

went out to meet Jethro, and did obeisance, and kissed him ; and they talked with one another of mutual " peace " or " welfare." The deed and the conversation demonstrate Peace in activity. A second illustration is from Zechariah.[1] The prophet has a vision of the Centre of the cosmos and its four winds. He is told to place the crown on the head of Joshua the son of Jehozedek, for he is a chosen King of Righteousness. The oracle tells that he shall be a priest upon his throne and shall compose Peace, that is the endemic linking up of man with man and them all with the Lord of Hosts. These two illustrations are noteworthy because of the Centre concept at the heart of them. The Shebat prophetical lection has, as we have seen, the same nucleus. Moreover, both would appeal to the writer of the Epistle as we shall see. They both serve to evoke the connotations of Peace as a spiritual architectonic of the psychic community.[2]

Its fellow in energy is Righteousness. There is nothing static about $Sedek$. There could not be in Rightness which is the essential Hebrew meaning of the word. From its simplest to its most spiritual usage, the word demands the community in which it works linkedly with Peace. For instance, a weight seems as if it could be nothing else but static. But the Semitic weight must be so used as to have a sense of the other person and of Jahwe.[3] The most formal of our notions of Righteousness springs from our ideas of law and

---

[1] vi, 1 ff.

[2] The name peace or welfare offering is eloquent of these things, from another point of view. In Exodus xxiv, 5, we see this being offered by members of the community and in its behalf.

[3] Leviticus xix, 36 ; Deuteronomy xxv, 15.

its administration. As soon as we touch this phase of the word we find that we must drop the formalising influences of Western practice. For the Semite, a judge is the agent of the oracles of Jahwe. He will maintain rightness between man and man ; but the spoken result is to be from Jahwe.[1] Equity is the maintenance of right balance of kinship between man and Jahwe. Isaiah has etched with a stroke or two this psychic community seeking the laws which should govern it : " They seek me daily and delight to know my ways : as a nation of right folk . . . they seek from me right laws, they delight to draw near unto Jahwe."[2] To place the king of such a community in his true part, we must turn to another Isaiah. He sets him upon the throne of the Centre in Jerusalem, and makes him to be the chief instrument of Jahvistic oracles. The seven-fold spirit of Jahwe informs him with what he shall say and do, " he shall not judge after the sight of his eyes, nor decide after the hearing of his ears." Rightness informs the whole community so that the very earth responds to its powers. All that can hurt or destroy passes away from the Centre of the cosmos.[3] Jeremiah sums up this matter in a name for the Centre ; " O dwelling-place of Rightness, O mountain of Wholeness,"[4] he exclaims. This is not a poetical name for any mountain. The prophet is naming the cosmical Centre the " homestead "[5] of the Rightness and Peace which vitalise the community. These are the

[1] Deuteronomy i, 16, xvi, 18 ; Proverbs viii, 15.
[2] Isaiah lviii, 2.
[3] Isaiah xi, 1 ff., xvi, 5.
[4] Jeremiah xxxi, 23 ; Isaiah i, 26.
[5] Cook, 397.

main meanings of Ṣedeḳ. Its energies unto vital Rightness in the community are twin energies with those unto its Peace. Without that Rightness there could be no Completeness. This equity is the *alter ego* of that equipoise in welfare. The psychic community has its being through the complemental and creative powers of Peace and Rightness.

The writer of the Epistle makes triumphant use of these Semitic ideas. At the close of chapter x he introduces two other names for Jesus Christ : " I shall be " and the Righteous. The first is a popular name for the Son of the Man which was known, for instance, to the disciples of John the Baptist and was brilliantly used in the service of Jesus Christ by the writer of the *Apocalypse*. Our writer presents this name by means of a tiny alteration of the text of Habbakuk ii, 3f. In the same manner he utilises the succeeding verse so that it yields the commanding name of the one whose function and nature is Ṣedeḳ.[1] His chief concern is with those names. He has forced them upon the text of the prophet. The fragments of original context which he retains are used by him for another purpose. He weaves them with the text of the Epistle to give nerve and strength to those who are ridden by the exiled mind. Immediately after he has given Jesus the name of the " King of Righteousness," for such is his intention, he writes chapter xi. That contains the moving and eloquent narrative of the psychic community. Its members live by faith. But " without us they should not be made perfect "—thus is the most

---

[1] Galatians iii, 25 makes a very different use of this verse. If Paul is drawing upon an anti-Judaic source ; Hebrews is certainly not doing so.

interesting verb τελειωθῶσιν rendered by the versions.
The writer is thinking in Hebrew though he is writing
in Greek. This verb is from the vocabulary of the
community. It stands for the verb form of Peace, the
companion phase of Rightness. An identical Hebrew
use of the verb to the Greek one in the Epistle is found
when Isaiah puts this question on the lips of Jahwe,[1]
" who is blind as the Lord's servant as he that is *at
peace* ? " The margin of the Revised Version adds in
its lexical manner, " or *made perfect*." Then the
words " with me " are added in the text to fill out the
question. Lexicons take on a theological tone when
they do the same thing. They suggest that the verb
covers the idea of a " covenant of peace " ; and with
a tone which suggests late Reformation theology rather
than Semitic philology. What the verse is really saying
is that this chosen man of Jahwe is not yet in entire
sensitive membership of the community. He is its
most significant member ; therefore he cannot be at
Peace until those senses are awake by which he receives
the oracles for the Peace of the whole of its members.
In the Epistle the sense of the verb has to do with the
entire spiritual establishment of the community. The
folk of faith without " the promise " and the folk of
faith with " the promise " create one society through
the Revealer. We shall observe the evangelical
significance of this conception when we deal with the
Maccabean factor in the Epistle. At present the
Semitic sociological phase of it must be kept in view.
Now the Hebrew word Peace has not been translated
into a Greek architectural or philosophical term.

[1] Isaiah xlii, 19.

The very Hebrew idea can be said to have been transliterated into Greek. It has taken on undreamt scope. That was bound to happen, when the Revealer was placed upon the throne of the concept of the psychic community. Through Him it has attained the Peace which is Entirety.

If this discovery is a true one, we ought to find that the great Hebrew idea has had other influence upon the Epistle. Two verses later, chapter xii, 2, are the familiar words, " looking unto Jesus, the author and perfecter of our faith." They compose a picture for most people of the Author who rests from His labours— a half-literary and half-exemplary picture of Him. Our writer, however, is recording two other names for Jesus which are not to be explained in the terms of his own craft. Jesus the one who makes entire or perfects has a name from the concept of Peace, which we have studied. He is architect and architectonic of the spiritual community. The first name of the two given Him here, ἀρχηγός, means " head of his house " or " people."[1] Do you not see how it demands those meanings of creative Peace for the second name ? The two are born of His connexions with His own community. An earlier statement in the Epistle, chapter ii, 10 ff., speaks of the Head of their salvation[2] made perfect through sufferings ; of the oneness of Sanctifier and sanctified ; of His participation in human conditions that He might overthrow Death[3] and

[1] Exodus vi, 14 ; Numbers x, 4, xiii, 3, xxv, 4 ; 1 Chronicles v, 24, viii, 28, xxvi, 26 ; Nehemiah vii, 70–1 ; Isaiah iii, 7.

[2] See Pedersen, 330 ff., for the community values of salvation.

[3] The writer has the same idea of embodied Death as the *Apocalypse*, xx, 2, etc.

deliver all who had been enslaved by him. The writer could scarcely have gone further in making clear the psychic community connotations of ἀρχηγός, unless he had used the actual phrase. Step by step he deepens and widens those connotations until they must body forth the society he depicts in chapter xi. Unless we watch him build up his idea of the community, we cannot seize with the power we should the emergence of Jesus as its High-Priest. And the significance of these names in chapter xii will be altogether eluded.

This concept of the High-Priest is, then, one which cannot be limited to the Lectionary of the Synagogue. The writer's inspirations are drawn as well from the people who were exiled from its use. To bring them spiritual repair he must lead them from the ancestral community which is in ruins to the community which cannot pass away. Ab and Tammuz represent the devastation of the former. Therefore the latter must have its bases sunk in its members' intellect and spirit. It must assuage the agonising demands which are in them. These looked out upon the world with *Maccabean* eyes, as we shall learn, and the tradition of Melchizedek was as it were the means through which they looked at Jesus Christ. From an influential figure in the community of which they were bereft, they looked out upon the indissoluble[1] community of " another High-priest."

Little progress is made with Melchizedek before we come upon the idea of " covenant." In such con-nexions are figure and idea that they suggest directly

---

[1] *Cf.* Hebrews vii, 17. This term surely has its significance from the community concept.

those of the origin and the originated. Thus in chapter vii, 22, a citation of Psalm cx is followed by the deduction, according to this Jesus has become the ensurer of the better covenant. A Maccabean Psalm is dominated by the figure of Melchizedek. He is the veritable embodiment of Rightness and Peace. His name and nature prove that.[1] He is all that we have found in the Semitic conceptions of those two terms alive and at work at the head of and in co-operation with the members of his community. We Westerners turn him into a hieratic and mystic forerunner of our ecclesiastical views of priesthood. Whereas he has nothing to say to us through the Epistle, if he does not embody and sensitively respond to the concept of the community ; and is himself the source of its Rightness and Completeness. The large place which the idea of a covenant has in conjunction with him loses the sense it had for its writer and his correspondents, if it is sundered from the creative energies of the community.

For a moment or two it will be well to illustrate the potency of a covenant in a Semitic society.[2] That the description potent is merited we may see from the phrase " covenant of Peace." Jahwe sets David as head over the house and himself as their divine over-head. That is a " covenant of Peace." It is one which is promised to last for ever. Institutionally, it centres about the sanctuary of Jahwe ; energetically, about the enthroned Son.[3] A covenant is essentially the *nexus*

[1] *E.g.*, Lods, *Israël des Origines au Milieu viiie. Siècle*, (1930) 149 ff. ; Johnson, 84 ff.

[2] Pedersen, 308 ff.

[3] *Cf.* Ezekiel xxxiv, 25, xxxvii, 26.

between the energies of Rightness and Completeness. It is to be thought of in terms of social life and not in those of contractual agreement. It had entity of its own which could be sent into a pillar of stone during covenant-making within the community.[1] " My covenant was life and peace " says Jahwe, for example, through the prophet Malachi.[2] A last illustration may be taken from the same prophet.[3] The community may cause its own corruption by slackening from the pursuit of Rightness and Peace. Then on some great festival day Jahwe will send a messenger, an " angel," of the covenant. In this instance it was to be Elijah. He will purge the members of the community as though gold and silver, then they will turn to offer sacrifices of Peace and Rightness.

Let us again remind ourselves that this fundamental of Semitic life and thought had been shattered twice in the first century. The immortal community, with its ritual centre, had been proved to be mortal. The use of this ritual centre, the Temple, is obvious. Chapter ix opens with the sanctuary of the first covenant and progresses towards the view of the new covenant and the perfect sanctuary at its centre. Chapter viii, by its use of Jeremiah xxxi, 31 ff., makes the ancient community with its " covenant of peace " ; and then causes it to be surpassed by the new community with its covenant which cannot wax old. Its High-Priest and King of Righteousness offers but one sacrifice, and therewith establishes His community in Peace and

---

[1] Genesis xxxi, 44 ff. ; Pedersen, 308.
[2] ii, 5.
[3] Malachi, iii, 2, iv, 5.

Rightness.[1] The animistic and primitive social values pass away, as does the sanctuary of stone, before the Son whose temple and energies unto Peace and Rightness in men are in the Eternal Spirit of God. Even the sounds of chaffering, which seem to linger in the Epistle's references to tithes, take on their true notes, when we understand that the subject had to arise from the writer's interest in the psychic community. Therein, tithes served to integrate its members in the social texture.[2] The Epistle takes this idea and shows how Abraham thus set himself in that one which went on through the ages. This conception of covenant, which is the vital bond between the energies that mould and perfect the community, is transformed by the presence of Revealer and revelation. Moses and Elijah, the messengers of a first covenant and community, are no more seen : Jesus only is seen with themselves.

Turning from the society to its traditional architect, we are in position to assess Melchizedek and Jesus Christ in accord with the Epistle's mode. His document, which is Psalm cx, has passed into the structure and substance of the whole of the Epistle. Not as a literal factor, but as a documentary and sociological inspiration which the Revealer has transformed. His contribution in bulk is of equal importance. Through him is set up a contrast with any who has had the name of angel or messenger (i, 13). He has lent Jesus his own name which set Him

---

[1] *Cf*. Hebrews x, 15 ff.
[2] *E.g.*, Numbers xviii, 21 ; Leviticus xxvii, 30 ; Deuteronomy xiv, 23, 28 ; 2 Chronicles xxxi, 5.

at the potent heart of the transformed Semitic community (v, 6, 10). And from his tradition our writer has recomposed the whole conception and energies of that community as the *organon* of the Revealer and His revelation (vii, 1 ff.). Thus for his correspondents, adrift from the immemorial fastnesses of Semitic community and temple, he brings the grace of a community which cannot pass away and whose liturgy is the revelation of Life through Jesus Christ our Lord. This he does in the terms of the most native possessions of the Semitic Folk-mind. These are transfigured by the revelation of Jesus Christ so that they can find natural access to that mind.

CHAPTER VI

THE HAVEN FOR EXILES IN THE LORD AND COMMUNITY
OF THE EPISTLE.

THE discovery of the place of the Semitic community
in the Epistle saves chapter xi from being thought of as
a large patch of rhetoric in a document of rare refine-
ment. But the writer's tact as an artist, and more
certainly still as a shepherd of exiles, would have
prevented such an empty area in his work. It is
proper to speak of this writer's tact rather than of his
taste. He serves beautiful truth and not beauty. His
sensitiveness as a thinker is his tact ; and he has
hidden a good deal of its refined work in the structure
of chapter xi. This use of documents and of Semitic
sociology has passed into its composition. The
first have become ministrants unto the exiled mind ;
and the second has become a picture of the society of
believers in the revelation of Jesus : an original
representation of " the body of Christ."

What has gone on that these Old Testament worthies
should be members of that body ? The lowlands have
not become highlands ; and therefore as by natural
process they have arrived. The slope of Sinai has not
imperceptibly graded into the easy rise of mount Zion.
The writer pictures them as going out to the revelation.

For him, God has never been other than Jesus revealed Him to be. Those folk are for ever, therefore they would come to Him in the larger areas of life. He has caused the concept of the psychic community to conquer time and space. That alone is an outstanding achievement.

Will you proceed to notice his exquisite sensibility of perception concerning the pilgrims' first step on that quest ? Follow down the folk enumerated in chapter xi, and ask again why they are there. Because his quick eye has detected the venture towards the city of God ; a better idea in primitive ritual ; a harlot's scarlet thread ; a move from Egypt to the Sinai desert ; a touch of vision in an old man's benediction— and the stories of the Jewish community have become the records of pilgrims unto God revealed in Jesus Christ. The writer has learnt of Him. He has watched how Jesus treated Nicodemus ; or overheard Him as he sat on the Samarian well-side ; or has treasured the story of the woman some men would have stoned. These are incidents in which the Revealer is listening for and wooing unto the first shy step of discipleship. From them our writer turns to put onward acts of Old Testament characters into the perspective of the immortal community of His disciples. Semitic sociology becomes an evangel for the folk who were thinking that the only deathless community had been shown by the Romans to be like dew upon the grass before a relentless sun.

This loveliness of workmanship is accomplished on a modest basis of documents. Rahab enters the elect company from thence. A study of chapter xi evinces

that down to verse thirty-two the writer chooses that
company from his Lectionary documents and their
subjects ; and because they meet the doubts and fears
of the exiled mind as it broods over the ruin of the
Semitic community. It is not then the gathered
momentum of what he has written which causes him
to continue after the question, " and what more shall
I say ? " He is not in a condition of literary breathless-
ness. His craftsmanship is too good that he should
have written such an impetuous fore-part of a chapter
that it had to go on. The power of the idea of the
community in the section which follows the question
is so strong as to demand the reason of some other
impact upon his mind : an influence which would
anneal the chapter as it stands.

Over seventy years ago Bleek[1] proved that the latter
part of chapter xi was inspired both in ideas and
language from 1 and 2 Maccabees. This view has
persisted down to Moffatt[2] who apparently used the
slightly enlarged findings on this subject by Delitzsch.[3]
These results are certain. There is now no call to
review them. We may notice in passing two matters of
vocabulary. These bind together more closely
chapters xi and xii. The latter opens with its reference
to the " dense cloud of witnesses." They are intent
upon the exiles' progress up to the testing-point when
the object of the quest is near. The writer uses the
descriptive term ἀγών. Now that is a Maccabean

---

[1] *Ueber die Stellung der Apokryphen des alten Testamentes im
Christlichen Kanon* (*Studien und Kritiken*, 1853), 339.

[2] 186 f.

[3] *Commentary on the Hebrews* (E.T. 1870), ii, 280 ff.

word. In those short writings which tell their remarkable story this term runs through its gamut of meanings, from games to ordeals of torture.[1] It would have been natural for him to borrow the word from the same source as that which gave him the term ἀρχηγός.[2] He would thus satisfy the economy of his workmanship. Moreover, a meaning for the word that was reminiscent of Maccabean fortitude, and which is crudely rendered as "race," would exactly carry on the burden and progress of his closing chapters. We can pass on from the discussion of assured things to investigate questions which as yet have no answers. For instance, why was chapter xi given the form it has ? Why have we such a processional bond between the two parts of this chapter as, " for the time would fail me if I tell of Gideon, Barak, Samson, Jephthe, David and Samuel and the prophets " ? Or why is there a Maccabean factor in the Epistle ?

Immediately before asking the question of what more should he say, our writer has set Rahab in her new glory of life. Why she is in the chapter we know. Lectionary and Revealer have borne her there. Her actual position, however, suggests that when the writer saw how she came to be at home in the greater spiritual community, he saw then how to construct his chapter from verse one to thirty-two. Her contribution to the maintenance of its Semitic shadow had given her place

---

[1] 2 Maccabees iv, 18 ; x, 28 ; xiv, 18, 43 ; xv, 9, 18 ; 4 Maccabees xi, 20 ; xiii, 15 ; xv, 29 ; xvi, 16 ; xvii, 11.

[2] See 1 Maccabees ix, 61 and especially x, 47, where the virtues of headship and of the community are extended to a Hellene : to his Jewish equals he " spake words of peace unto them and they remained confederate with him always."

in the body of the Christian society. It was easy for
him to bring the others home after she was safe. Thus
the chapter down to the question went together with
natural ease. But Rahab would not suggest the
continuity of the community to the exiled mind.
Liberation for it on this vital subject could be accomplished only as the writer showed that the nuclear men
of the old community were equally within the new
society. Therefore he recites the names of the judges
of the elder society. We have been content to look
upon them as names in a roll-call of Israelitish heroes.
They are more than soldiers. Their place in the line
of nuclear men, as we have described them, gives them
right to be in chapter xi. David ends the line, it will be
noticed ; and he is the eponymous king-priest of the
community's monarchical period.

What is meant by nuclear men ? Men who are
central to the organism of the community, as we have
already found it to be : the resonant instruments of
Jahwe, as we have seen they were. Four of these men
are recorded in the Book of the Judges. It will be
well to collect thence information as to their ways and
work. Jahwe manifested himself to them.[1] He
informed them spiritually.[2] They were made as
bodily robes for his spirit.[3] " The spirit of Jahwe
rushed upon " them ;[4] then they spake and did with

[1] Judges vi, 11 ff.
[2] xi, 29.
[3] vi, 34.
[4] xiv, 19. Some agree that this is a gloss, *e.g.*, Van Doorninck,
Bidjrage tot de Tekskritiek van Richterin i–xvi (1879) ; Burney,
The Book of Judges (1920), *ad loc*. It is at least a contemporary
view of how a deliverer was equipped ; see xiv, 6.

I

might.   Of the two who are unrecorded in that book, Samuel from a child was said to be sensitive to the revelation and voice of Jahwe.[1] When Samuel anointed David before the people, we read " the spirit of the Lord came mightily upon "[2] him.   Following this code of primary significances for the judges, we can understand why " the prophets " are mentioned with them in Hebrews xi, 32.   This union also serves to discriminate who and what are meant by the seemingly familiar designation.   The writer is not covering the whole of the Old Testament, as if he were holding the view that the aisles of the Jewish Church were merging into those of the Christian Church.   He had not read Dean Stanley.   He is controlled in chapter xi by the concept of the community.   The virtues of the judges he has named are, for instance, communal virtues.   Their office and qualities, which are primarily to communicate the spirit of Jahwe to their fellows by deed and word or to ensure its sovereignty throughout the society, prove them to be such.   We had seen this before in part ; now we can perceive it wholly.   The prophets then should be the same sort of men as the judges.

This conclusion leads to an illuminating distinction. There are primitives and moderns among the prophets : they who follow the early modes of inspiration and those who have surpassed them.   Ezekiel went back to the former ways.[3]   That is a principal reason why

[1] 1 Samuel iii, 9, 21, etc.

[2] 1 Samuel xvi, 13.   That the Davidic king-priest was also judge, see e.g., Isaiah, xi, 3.

[3] E.g., Ezekiel ii, 2, iii, 24, xi, 5. See Buttenwieser, *Hebrew Union College Annual* (1930), 11 ff., on this distinction.

he reconstructed Jerusalem of the world's Centre, both
in institutions and legislation.[1]   In the ancient manner
he had become ears and eyes and vital bringer of Peace
to " the house of Israel " : a true Head of the community. There is the difference between him and
Jeremiah, for example. It is also the difference which
the writer to the Hebrews has in mind when he puts
" the prophets " after the names of the psychic
judges.[2] It is the organic community that matters
in chapter xi.

Thus a literary pointer is offered us when we begin
to wonder if after all chapter xi is a complexity rather
than a unity. For does not the writer go on to use
Maccabean material ? What part could it have with
the psychic community ? These are legitimate
questions. The beginning of an answer is troubled
by the fact that the style of 1 Maccabees is of a rather
stiff epistolary order. Therefore in it we may not
expect definite expression of the primitive status of
priest-kingship. It is right to believe that such
ideas are beneath the surface of its chapters. Portions
of the book touch the Epistle too closely that its writer
should have to reduce the chief notions he sought from
modern formalities to primitive conditions. When,
for instance, the narrative of the last words of
Mattathias[3] is compared with chapter xi, it is difficult

[1] See especially his document for the Feast of Tabernacles,
xl–xlviii.
[2] Cf., The offices of *Kahin* in prehistoric Islam ; Lammens,
L'Arabie Occidentale avant l'Hégire (1928), 106 ff. Also Daniel
iii, 2 f., where judge and soothsayer are equated. The primitive
Israelitish idea in that equation is unaffected by the suggestion
that the word in Daniel is possibly a Persian one.
[3] 1 Maccabees ii, 49 ff.

to avoid the conclusion that the general form of the
chapter has in that narrative its immediate exemplar.
Near to the narrative in 1 Maccabees ii, occurs the
statement, most striking in its sturdiness, of this
noble priest-king's regard for the community and its
covenant of Peace.[1] This makes another reason for its
influence on the Epistle. A third illustration stands
out from this same portion of 1 Maccabees. After
Mattathias had slain the apostate at the altar, he called
unto those who would maintain the covenant to flee
with him to the mountains. And we are told that
" many who were seeking righteousness and judgment
went down to abide there, they and their sons, and their
wives and cattle."[2] There is large reason for saying
that this is not Semitic ethics but civics : the pursuit
of Peace and Rightness for the community and not the
attainment of the raw material of theology. When
these things are added together, the conclusion is
irresistible that our writer had found in the Maccabean
factor not only a primary influence as to the form of
chapter xi, but also the unifying influence of its thought.
This in 1 Maccabees, as we have seen, pressed upon the
ideas of the community and its psychic upkeep unto
Peace and Rightness. In the Hebrews, we must
notice, the progress of ideas is through the processional
parenthesis to these immediately succeeding phrases :
" who through faith subdued kingdoms, wrought
righteousness, obtained promises." That is the
rendering of our standard translations.

The accepted view of those phrases is that the

[1] 1, ii, 17 ff.
[2] 1, ii, 27 ff.

writer is referring to military prowess and its results.
That commits him to tautology. For he concludes
this cluster of phrases with, " waxed mighty in war,
turned to flight armies of aliens." He was not so poor
an artist that within the space of nine short phrases he
would repeat himself. They too make up a catalogue
of the virtues of the men who pass by in his parenthesis.
It would be unnecessary that he should over-record
their fighting qualities. That he began his list with
other than these we can be sure. Since if we glance
into the Book of Judges, for example, we shall soon
find that even waxing mighty in battle was a judicial or
priestly function rather than a warrior's privilege. The
spirit of Jahwe, both in the man and the community, is
the inspiration and the reason for his deeds. Therefore
it is probable that all of the nine virtues ought to be
envisaged within the idea of the community. Let
us test this view on the more familiar-looking of the
first two phrases—" wrought righteousness."

It is interpreted as yielding a theological commonplace. Let Rightness be put into the place of the
word which has led to that result. The phrase begins
to look as if it had new significance. Moulton[1] has
remarked upon its verb that it " surveys in perspective
the continuous labour." This verb is applied to work
upon a material or a man or to building and tilling.
Then the writer surely has cut a cameo two words large
to represent the sculpturing work of Jahwe's man unto
Rightness in the community. What of its neigh-
bouring phrase " subdued kingdoms " ? Its verb has

[1] *A Grammar of New Testament Greek, Prolegomena*
(1906), i, 116.

the same perspective significance. A process is reviewed and completed. We too should remind ourselves that its noun has for its root meaning the abstract conception of sovereignty.[1] Indeed, we thrust it into concrete conditions : we consider that the writer means the overthrow of kingdoms other than the Israelitish society. It is not a literary crime to repeat things. It is only a needless charge at this point in the Epistle. The contending of the verb implies spiritual effort. The noun carries the notion of " sovereignties." S. Paul lends an illustration of what is meant. He causes Jesus Christ to render up sovereignty to God, " when he shall have abolished all rule and all authority and power."[2] Those last three terms represent other forms of sovereignty ! Paul is talking Eschatology, and on the scale of a world. Hebrews is talking Sociology, first, on the scale of a Semitic community ; and, then, on that of the Christian society. Paul must abolish universally : Hebrews must subdue communally. One is concerned with the *finale* of the mortal : the other is taken up with the realisation of the concept of Semitic Peace in the immortal community. Then these first two phrases of verse thirty-four gain their original meaning by being put back into the vital man of the Semitic society.

Once more we are made to come upon the ideas unto which the writer and his pen are obedient. Therefore the other items in the list of virtues should be dealt with. The wonder-working ones need no

---

[1] Moulton and Milligan, *Vocabulary of the Greek Testament* (1915), ii, 104.
[2] 1 Corinthians xv, 24.

annotation. A man could not be the agent of Jahwe's spirit without the attribution of such qualities. We come again to the last two descriptive phrases, "waxed mighty in war, put to flight armies of aliens." It has been said already that these represent functions of the man at the heart of the community. Samuel as judge and priest in Mizpah, having at his service the thunder of Jahwe, and then putting the Philistines to flight,[1] is a true illustration of what those phrases mean. Ezekiel has both allegorised and argued the theory of the matter.[2] For a theory is implied ; seeing that any act of these men would not be external to the community, but would have concern with its covenant. The allegory of the eagle resplendent with many colours and of the top of the cedar tree with its botanical versatility will be recalled by the readers of the prophet. Argument is made whether members of a Semitic community can be gathered into a covenant of Peace should they be overcome by an alien power. This attempted evacuation of what is an essentially Jahvistic society is proved to be an impossibility. It would be the radical flouting of its organic relationships. What of the converse position ? Can aliens be incorporated into the community ?[3] Joshua was facing the kings of the Jordan hill-country and of the Lebanon sea-front. Out of fear the Gibeonites disguised themselves, and came to cajole Joshua into making covenant with them. They deceived him. He admitted them to the Peace of the community. Their ruse was found out. They could not be killed because they had been admitted ;

[1] I Samuel vii, 5 ff.
[2] Ezekiel xvii.
[3] *Cf.* Pedersen, 292 ff.

so they were turned into ritual slaves.[1] Because of the
error committed, they had to be subordinate not to a
racial organisation but to a ritual organism. It had to
be kept and made entirely intact. It had also to be
supreme ritually. The force of arms might be used
to establish either or both conditions ; but in so doing
they would be Jahvistic agencies wielded by Jahwe's
chosen men in behalf of social Peace and Rightness.
These two virtues have now their right meanings.
By them the unity of the structure and thought of
chapter xi is maintained. They also include the
Maccabean factor with structural care. For the
Maccabees were of this type of warrior ; that is, judge-
priests in the panoply of defence for the sake of the
spiritual community.

The possession of those connotations has caused the
Maccabean factor to shape the first thirty verses of
chapter xi. Other details of its epic have inspired the
writer's narrative down to the close of this chapter,
where is the notable declaration of the psychic community. Lest a suspicion should arise that our
investigation of the Epistle has yielded too much to
that intriguing designation, we must connect up what
has been found for chapter xi with the main ideas of
chapter xii.

The chapter opens and ends superbly. Between
these two literary heights is a space of fourteen verses
long. The strong tendency of the commentators is to
consider that the writer is building a bridge between

[1] Joshua ix. Concerning Deut. xxiii, 8–9, see Morgenstern
H.U.C.A. (1935), 129. 211, who points out that the Egyptians,
whose children were to be admitted into the Semitic community
in the third generation, were " Egyptian Jews or half-Jews."

them with a moral—a rather insubstantial bridge. He ought, of course, to have his valley experiences of thought. Of set purpose he may put literary and spiritual valleys in his Epistle. He would have to if he is to follow the workings of the exiled mind. But he nowhere moralises : he everywhere vitalises. We can and do sometimes make him into a banal thinker. He will be reduced to that condition when we omit to seek the founts of his ideas and their ministry to his correspondents. This space, composed of verses three to seventeen, has its living connexions with the Epistle's creative ideas and structure.

We must remind ourselves that the opening of chapter xii has its specific Maccabean notes as to vocabulary, and its community notes as to ideas. By these two influences Jesus Himself is named and interpreted. He is Head and Perfecter of the House of Faith ; and as such He lived and endured the cross. Let us at once relieve our writer from the burdensome charge of writing a theory of the crucifixion. He has one aim, which is the aim of the whole Epistle—to heal and win the exiled mind. It struggles and complains : it yields to the Silent Voices. It is not chidden for forgetting certain maxims of morality but for disregarding the basis of communal vitality. His plea for sonship takes them back to that. To make his point he cites a piece of Proverbs iii. A curious choice, it seems at first, for one who so largely uses the Synagogal Lectionary. This feeling goes when we recall that his Jeremiah citation in chapter viii came to him because of its literal relations with one of the Torah Lections which has deeply influenced his work.

If we read the next verse to the one which concludes
his citation, we come upon the likely prompter of his
choice of the Proverbs passage. Jeremiah xxxi, 18,
memorably uses the word which we commonly translate
as " chastened." Our writer has reacted to the
Greek word and not to its Jeremaic meaning. We do
him wrong if we allow the Proverbs context to this
word to set its meaning. Its " scourge " will certainly
start our minds after another parental sophism about
sparing the rod. He cites a passage for a word's sake
as he has done for a name's sake. The stress he lays
upon this word is a future one. What is being done is
towards participation in the divine wholeness and the
yielding of Peace and Rightness [1] Polybius has the
word in question, and it bears the sense " to be given a
good lesson for the future."[2] That is too scholastic
to fit the Hebrews. It has, however, the forward look
which is a phase of the meaning required by the
Epistle. Its full sense is there marked out by what is
to be shared and yielded. These are fruits of the
community, its completed ends. As energies they
make both members and society. Thus, too, they will
perfect the whole. Will you notice that the Epistle
almost writes the designation " psychic community."
It puts the thing even more concisely, " in subjection
to the Father of spirits."[3] This title calls up the

---

[1] Hebrews xii, 11, καρπὸν εἰρηνικὸν δικαιοσύνης.

[2] Polybius, ii, 9, 6 ; Moulton and Milligan (1926), vi, 474.

[3] Hebrews xii, 9. Moffatt, 203, refers to 2 Maccabees iii, 24,
and describes its use of the term as " Hellenistic Judaism." He
goes on to refer to the use of the title " Lord of spirits " and
remarks that in Hebrews xii, 9 " spirits cannot here mean angels."
They, of course, are unwanted. His treatment at this point is
due to his ideas of hellenised Judaism.

Maccabean one, "the Sovereign of spirits."[1] The two have the same essential meaning. It is notable that our writer shaped his on the Maccabean analogue. The unusual statement which contains it helps to evoke the communal context of the writer's thought as far as we have gone.

There remain verses fourteen to seventeen. Are they merely platitudinous ? Does Esau carry more than a warning about behaviour ? It seems difficult to make more of the injunction, "follow after peace with all men," which is its standard rendering, than a genial and harmless condition of neighbourliness. But that piece of advice blurs the original meaning and erases the original shape of the sentence. A sentimental universalism extrudes every Semitic feature and destroys its circumference. Our writer is dealing with those who would "fall away from" the society of disciples. Each member had to seek its Peace in such manner that none is defiled. Illicit or profane union like that of Esau fractures the community. But how is this done ? The blessing of the dying head of a community meant a transference of his spirit and powers to the one blessed : "that my soul may bless thee" said Isaac.[2] The firstborn became the nuclear man of the House. He was and wrought in miniature what the Davidic head was and wrought in the vast Israelitish society. Our writer's bright and leal mind could not condone acts which would break the inheritance, whether in the old or the new society. Each member of the latter was called upon to remember

---

[1] 2 Maccabees iii, 24.
[2] See Pedersen on this subject, 200.

that he was as a firstborn to the Firstborn of God : an inheritor of the birthright within the immortal community. The immemorial laws of the Semitic community disinherited the breaker of its covenant with irrevocable precision. Their automatic irrevocability passed into the writer's judgment when he thought of the disinherited Christian Semite : the one who had gone back to the lowland ways behind him. Hebrews vi, 6, says how impossible it is "to renew them again unto repentance " : Hebrews xii, 17, says of the disinherited Esau " he was rejected, he found no place of repentance."

That is a notable return to a major conclusion and its terms which appeared in the middle of the Epistle, vi, 6. It is clear evidence of the unity of the writer's thought and of the control exercised over the whole of his work by the idea of the Semitic community. This was inevitable. The exiled mind and the great Fasts had that as their chief preoccupation. It will be well to illustrate this further from the prophetical lections for the Fast of Tammuz ; both because of what we have done and of the other material in the Epistle which has yet to be examined. For instance, Jeremiah i portrays the judge-priest become the prophet. It was no great step for him to take. Jahwe touches his lips : " I have put my words in thy mouth." With them he was " to build and to plant." Within the community that was his work : without by their power he might " cast down and destroy." Then function, achievements and areas of work are the same as those ascribed by the Epistle to the earlier judges. Another example is Isaiah lvi, 1-8. It pictures the community at Peace and with Rightness. The enfolding life is so strong in it that Jahwe says : " Neither let the proselyte, that hath joined himself to the Lord, speak, saying, the Lord will surely separate me from his people : neither let the eunuch say, Behold I am a dry tree." Even the man who is added to the original spiritual membership of the society, or the man who is physically sterilised from its social maintenance is enmeshed in its web of life. This alive community is depicted as gathered about the Centre of the cosmos, the Mount in Jerusalem. And Jahwe promises to perfect the community in these words, " I will gather others to his own gathered ones." The only necessary comment is to remark on the power of these lections to stimulate memory and desire in Semitic people. The sensitive intellect of our writer would be bound to react to them. Even apart from the Maccabean factor, he would have had to compose his Epistle as he has done and submit to the monarchy of the concept of the community. These compulsions would become overwhelming when to them was added the new-born concept of the society of the disciples of Jesus Christ which like Himself could never die. The illustrations carry back confirmation for our findings ; they also look forward to the close of the Epistle. They compose for it a second preface. Its greater preface is the whole of the document. Before these matters can be gone into, we must discover the final reasons why the Epistle has a Maccabean factor. They too will answer the more fundamental question why there is an Epistle to the Hebrews and what was its destination.

Concerning the Maccabean factor, there can be no doubt that its literature could find no place in the Jewish Lectionary. Our analysis has accounted for certain Psalms which are present in the Epistle. They fit the factor which is at work in its structure and thought. Further, the reason for the presence of Melchizedek has been traced to the fact that his tradition was appended to the Maccabean epic. He was there because he was the founder of city and temple. To this point the factor could be described as a purely literary one. That would not, however, explain all the facts of its influence. Melchizedek comes in the train of the Maccabees. They do not come in his. In turn, they would have no place in the Epistle if it were not for the Fast of Ab. The calendrical direction of " 5 Maccabees " is a small but a precious piece of evidence. Then it must be demonstrated that somewhere the month of Ab and the Maccabees are united by a powerful religious bond. It will be potent enough to have inspired the writer to compose his Epistle, marshal his sources and set himself to evangelise the exiled mind—and simply because the bond is coupled with that month. These conditions presuppose as well that this component must have had such spiritual eminence in the area where his exiles were living, that it represented both the utter fascination of the ways behind them and the noble basis of appeal to the ways before them.

All ancient evidence points to Antioch as the centre of religious interest in the Maccabees. Jewish and

Christian cult had its site there. Jerome[1] is the sole instance of doubt concerning the claims of Antioch. His surprise is resolved when we recognise that by his time the Christian cult of the Maccabees was established and had spread in Palestine. The express claims of Chrysostom,[2] the celebrated Antiochian, and of Augustine[3] who knew the basilica of Antioch, are more than enough to outweigh his half-hearted *caveat*. They too are upheld by evidence both before and after their date. The pre-Christian evidence, which is notably presented in 2 Maccabees vi and vii, has been proved to have no reference to Jerusalem but to Antioch as the place of martyrdom. Since Cardinal Rampolla's[4] investigation and down to Dom Leclercq's recent article,[5] that is the established opinion.[6] Antioch is the shrine of the Maccabees. It is vain to question

[1] *De Situ et Nominibus Locorum Hebraicorum* (ed. Verona, 1735), iii, 247–250, Modein or Μηδεειμ ; *cf.* Modim, *Comm. in Isaiam*, Lib. ix, xxx (iv, 402). Plainly the emphasis in Jerome's statement should fall on the underlined word : " quorum (*i.e.*, Maccabees) *hodeique* ibidem sepulcra monstrantur."

[2] *Hom.* i, *Patr. Gr.* L, 618 ff., *Hom.* ii, 525 ff., *Hom.* iii, 626 ff., Gregory Naz., *Orat.* xv, xxxv, 912 ff. For the Syriac version of this sermon see Bensly and Barnes cited *infra*, where it is the first document in their book.

[3] *Sermo* ccc, *Patr. Lat.* xxxviii, 1376 ff. *Sermo* ccci, 1380 ff. See also Ambrose, *Ep.* xl, 16, *P.L.* xvi, 1107 ; Gaudentius, *Sermo* xv, xx, 948 ff. ; Leo, *Sermo* xix, liv, 517 ff., a document attributed to this pope ; Maximus Taurinensis, *Sermo* lxxix, lvii, 691 ff., *Sermo* lxxx, 693 ff., *Sermo* lxxxiii, 697 ff. ; Prudentius, *Peristephanon* v, 523 ff., x, 776 ff. (ed. Bergman, *C.S.E.L.*, lxi, 1926).

[4] *Bessarione* (1897), 655 ff. ; (1898) 9 ff.

[5] Cabrol and Leclercq, *Dictionnaire*, i, ii, 2375 ff.

[6] Delehaye, *Les Origines du Culte des Martyrs* (1933), 201 f.; Thurston and Attwater, ed. Butler, *Lives of the Saints* (1933), viii, 7, lay too much stress on Jerome ; the latter say his statement " defies solution."

her right. Fresh support for her claims and also for
the Maccabean factor in the Epistle can be gained by
a new examination of this matter. It may seem as if
we are taking a by-path. We shall find that thus we
come to the end of the highway of our principal
subject.

For a short while we must turn from the study of the
Epistle to that of ancient Calendars and Martyrologies.
On the Christian side, these alone offer documentary
evidence for the Antiochian connexions of the
Maccabees. They are, however, the moulds for
lectionaries and liturgies. A Mass for these saints is
in one old Service Book, the Gelasian Sacramentary ;[1]
and a *Preface* is in another, the Gregorian Sacramentary.[2] These are Roman compositions.[3] They did
not come with the saints from Palestine. It is as
possible to discriminate what is Palestinian and
what is Roman among the material of Calendars and
Martyrologies. That is their chief value for our
purpose.

There is only one starting-point for our quest. That
is the Syriac Martyrology whose date is 411 A.D.[4] It
is the most important documentary discovery yet made
for the critical study of early Calendars and
Martyrologies. Two views of it hold the field. The
first says that it is an abridged copy of the Hieronymian

---

[1] Muratori, *Liturgia Romana Vetus* (1748), i, 658.

[2] Wilson, *The Gregorian Sacramentary* (*Henry Bradshaw
Society*, xlix, 1915), 282.

[3] Frere, *Studies in Early Roman Liturgy* (1930), i, 127.

[4] Wright, *Journal of Sacred Literature* (1866), 45 ff.; Nau
Patr. Or. (1915), x, 7 ff.

Martyrology;[1] the second says that it is an abridgment of the Nicomedian Martyrology.[2] The former is the well-known Latin document; the latter is a reconstructed Greek document. It is held that it is a source of the Latin work. As to its character, it is a gathering of early Oriental martyrs and saints. This swift summary of critical views leads us directly to the testing of the qualities of the Syrian Martyrology. The entry in it which is of surpassing interest to us is : " First of the month of Ab, according to the Greeks, the confessors—the sons of Samouna, known as the Maccabees—who are among those buried at Antioch in the Kerateum."

For its own sake and the Epistle's some remarks must be made on this entry. The phrase " according to the Greeks " refers of course only to the date. The term " confessors " is another word for " martyrs " as Severus tells us in one of his *Cathedral Sermons* preached at Antioch.[3] Now that time-phrase is used on nine occasions in the Syrian Martyrology. Its plain meaning then is that the Syrian writer is doing just what a bilingual man would do : he is referring to certain matters which in his native Syriac would be put differently. We shall gain light for the Maccabean entry by looking into the other occurrences of the

[1] Duchesne, *Les Sources du Martyrologe Hiéronymien* (*Mélanges d'Archéologie et d'Histoire*, 1885), 122 ff. *Cf.* Delisle, *Bibliothèque de l'École des Chartes* (1894), 425 f.

[2] Delehaye, *Analecta Bollandiana* (1913), 369 ff. ; *Cf.* Lawlor, *The Psalter and Martyrology of Ricemarch.* (*Henry Bradshaw Society*, xlvii, 1914), xxv ff. Leclercq in Cabrol, *Dictionnaire*, x, ii, 2571, thinks the Oriental Martyrology was derived from Eusebius and in Nicomedia.

[3] Severus, *Hom. Cathedrales*, liii (ed. Duval, *Patr. Or.*, iv, 1908), 22.

K

phrase. For instance, on October 2, it is used concerning a Nicomedian saint; on November 8, of a Cappadocian confessor; on December 26, of a Jerusalemite martyr; on April 2, of a group of Thessalonican saints; on July 15, of a saintly bishop of Nisibis.[1] It is needless to take up the other examples. These that are cited can mean only what has been claimed as to their usage of the time-phrase. The writer could not have been abridging the so-called Nicomedian Martyrology, no matter the language in which it is said to have been composed. It, as we have noticed, would form a register of the religious heroes of the Near East. Such a document is not implied by the phrase " according to the Greeks." The Syrian author of the Martyrology in question could not have borrowed from a Nicomedian or Oriental Martyrology an entry about a Nicomedian saint, and have prefaced it with that phrase. Any more than he could have done the same for the entries of a martyr of Jerusalem and of a Syrian bishop. To conclude otherwise is to ignore the simple but influential fact of his bilingual condition.

When we turn to the Maccabean entry with these considerations in mind, a more important conclusion emerges. For certain of the entries in his book, the Syrian is thinking in one calendar, which is native to him, and writing in another, which is not native to him. It is indubitable that the Palestinian Folk-calendar had as its Maccabean date the 9th of Ab. That is the first day of the Jewish Fast. Thence came

---

[1] Leclercq, x, ii, 2563, appears to believe that this July entry is a solitary addition by a Syriac hand. This opinion ignores the true conditions of the document's composition.

the Greek motive for putting it down as the first day of
August. A Hebrew Fast first day had become a Greek
calendrical first day. There is early and late ecclesiastical unanimity as to this last date.[1] The Syrian's
phrase, therefore, is without reason if it does not mean
that he is aware of the Palestinian date and its
transference to another place and significance by
those who are not Palestinians. There is little room for
doubt that the author of the Syrian Martyrology has
knowledge of the earliest, and most probably unwritten,
Calendar which in historical outline preserved the
native story of the Church of Jesus Christ.

[1] De Rossi and Duchesne, *Martyrium Hieronymianum* (*Acta
Sanct.*, Nov. ii, 1894), lix, lxxi, 99 ; Fasti of Polemius Sylvius,
C.I.L., i, 271 ; Calendar of Carthage (*Acta*, Nov. ii, 1, lxx ff.). And
e.g., *The Calendar of S. Wilibrord*, 10 and fol. 38 (Wilson, *Henry
Bradshaw Society*, lv, 1918) ; *English Kalendars before A.D.*1100
(Wormold, *H.B.S.*, lxxii, 1934), i, 23, 37, 51, 65, 79, 93, 107, 121,
135, 149, 163, 177, 191, 205, 219, 233, 247 ; Lawlor *supra*. Also
Herzfeld, *An Old English Martyrology* (*Early English Text
Society*, Series i, 116 ; 1900), 132 f. This is a document in eighth-
century Mercian dialect, and is recognised as having Near
Eastern connexions (xxxiv f.). Of about the same date is *The
Martyrology of Oengus the Culdee* (Stokes, *H.B.S.*, xxix, 1905),
174, which also may have oriental connexions. There is some
uncertainty in the Roman Lectionary as to the proper Gospel for
the day of the Maccabees. Frere, *Studies in Early Roman Liturgy*
(1934), ii, 181 (Mt. xii, 46–50), 195 (Mt. xiv, 22–33), thus records
two lections. In the Melchite Lectionary, Mt. x, 16 ff., is said to
be the proper lesson (Bensly and Barnes, xxi). These variations
do not affect the unanimity as to the date August 1. Nor in any
way does the view that the lections in the Roman Breviary have
been annexed to the order of the Jewish solar calendar. This has
been illustrated by the coincidence of lections from Maccabean
literature and the events of the Jewish feast of Hanukkah
(Venetianer, *Zeitschrift der deutschen morgenländischen Gesell-
schaft*, 1909, 145 ; Rankin, *The Festival of Hanukkah* in Hooke,
The Labyrinth, 1935, 196). 1 Maccabees is read on the first
Sunday in October and 2 Maccabees on the fourth. These can
have nothing to do with the feast. The origin of the Roman
calendar is an independent problem.

It is worth while going a little farther along the by-way which leads to the end of our highway. The martyr of Jerusalem who, " according to the Greeks," is celebrated on December 26, is none other than S. Stephen. This date also has universal currency. The oldest Syrian and Armenian Calendars, for instance, uphold it. That makes the later Syrian evidence doubly certain, since the Armenian was the direct inheritor of the Syrian Church. This evidence then is the same as that covered by the phrase " according to the Greeks." The writer also thus describes it as once more shown to be dependent upon a primary and native historical source. Did this date, December 26, arise in the same way as August 1 ? It has been suggested that Stephen was made a martyr on a day of Jewish festival, either Pentecost or Tabernacles.[1] The narrative of Acts of the Apostles vii offers little or no support for either of those suggestions. But Stephen's witness before his persecutors actually quotes the prophetical lection for the first Sabbath in Shebat, that is Isaiah lxvi. Moreover, the only other citation he makes, as the record informs us, which is Amos v, 25 to 27, is simply a more vivid presentation of what Isaiah says in lxvi, 17. The Acts marks the Palestinian day of the martyrdom by reference to the Lectionary of the Synagogue.[2] It is an arresting fact that just as the non-

---

[1] Lagrange, *Saint Etienne et son sanctuaire à Jérusalem* (1894), 27, 2.

[2] The Epistle, for example, has offered us more than one reason why this should be looked upon as the expected method in New Testament writings.

Palestinian date for the Maccabees was got by moving time back seven days, thus also was S. Stephen's day reckoned. In this way, light is thrown upon the compiling of the chronology which has influenced all succeeding ecclesiastical Calendars.

The fifth century Syrian Martyrology, therefore, can contain much earlier material. It would be a quaint document if it could not. Duchesne has carried back certain of its contents to 363.[1] Our findings go still farther back. They disclose the first chronicles of the nascent Church. The *Epistle to the Hebrews* presents the Judæo-Christian inspirations for the rise of the Maccabean cult. These are met by a Syrian notice of the cult which is markedly Antiochian in detail. That sort of evidence is unique in the Syrian Martyrology. This detail also has independent support solely in writers who knew Antioch : a native historian and scholar[2] and a student of the city's antiquities. These matters and the uniqueness of the entry suggests that the Martyrology was written by a native of Antioch. We are shepherded every way to that city as the centre of the cult of the Maccabees. A conclusion which, when viewed together with all the evidence laid bare, contributes decisively to the view that the Epistle was written to those in Antioch who, in the period near to

---

[1] Duchesne, *Mélanges*, 127.

[2] John Malalas, *Chronographia*, viii, 207 (ed. Dindorff, 1831). This writer not only supports the Martyrology as to the quarter of the city in which the Maccabees were buried, but adds the valuable detail that the tombs were near the Synagogue of Antioch.

the destruction of the Temple and the rise of the 9th of Ab,[1] were turning themselves to the wizardry of the lowland ways and the Silent Voices. Its writer will have been a man of the type of Barnabas.[2] It looks as if Time itself is against the idea, a captivating one, of Barnabas being the actual author of the Epistle.

One other Antiochian document ought to have its place in the investigation of the Epistle, and at this point. It was copied in Antioch itself in the eleventh century, a homiletic document in Syriac.[3] The Maccabean martyrdoms are set by it in that city. That is an original note. Another is the reason it gives for their death. They died because they honoured Jesus Christ the Saviour. The usual reasons of the martyrologies do not appear. A third original note is in the actual citation of the Epistle by the mother of the Maccabees at the end of her witness. These features are lit with the fresh light of significance from all that we have found concerning the Epistle. Barnes, who edited Bensly's transcript of the Syriac document, thought that the whole was a hasty attempt to make a Jewish story into a Christian tract. He was writing

[1] As to the date of the rise of the Fast, see Thackeray, 83 : " in the years following, A.D. 70."

[2] Acts xi and xiii. My findings lead me again to doubt that chapter xiii, with its use of Timothy's name, could have belonged to the original Epistle. The telescoping of a lost Pauline Epistle with *To the Hebrews* would offer an adequate reason why the whole should have been ascribed to Paul.

[3] Bensly and Barnes, *The Fourth Book of Maccabees and Kindred Documents in Syriac* (1895), the fourth of the documents published by them.

two years before Rampolla had established Antioch as the site of the martyrdoms. His opinion, therefore, reflects the accepted one of his time that at Jerusalem the Maccabees had been put to death. There is no ground for his opinion in the claim that the scribe has changed the name of the mother, Samouna, into Mary on several occasions, but not on all. That seems to be the sole eleventh-century feature of the document. The scribe, like his annotator nearly nine hundred years after him, overlooked the first-century conception of the Maccabees. They were of the immortal community of Jesus Christ. The early realisation of this fact could only have arisen in Antioch. It is that which now trickles into expression through the mesh of the earlier Jewish narrative of the Maccabees. The copyist tried to stay its flow : his editor almost succeeded. But the opening of the document states their allegiance to Jesus Christ : the end cites one of the most significant things in the Epistle, that they looked for the well-founded city whose builder and creator is God. Its opening is Hebrews xii, 1 to 13, in fine austerity of epitome ; and its close is the most appropriate use of Hebrews xi, 10. It is suggested then that these features point to natural preservation of early Antiochian material, and not to an Antiochised mediæval document. That the scribe copies an older document, and is not creating a view of the Maccabees which is without source. Long before the eleventh century, Palestinian commentators had settled down to a received view of the Epistle. Then these gleams of earliest opinion can only belong to a period close to their rise.

It seems a charming and natural touch that an eleventh-century scribe should have attempted to name Samouna after Mary the Mother. Perhaps, however, that was not his reason for the arrested change. He may have known and have been influenced by the Hieronymian Martyrology in one of its later forms, such as are represented by its three typical manuscripts. Thus, for instance, if he turned over its pages to the entry for *iiii. Id. Aug.* he would find a Mary mentioned there " with vi others," as the two eighth-century manuscripts record.[1] Or if he turned back a month or two to *xv. Kal. Ap.*, he would see another Mary's name following upon this phrase, " with vii others."[2] That is to say, the scribe was beguiled into writing the name Mary upon his under-script by the number of Samouna's children. Whether the former or latter reason for the partial change be accepted, it is plain that it alone belongs to the mediæval copyist.

Therefore, these broken gleams of evidence project, though dimly, that stage of the Christian cult of the Maccabees in Antioch which followed upon the creative inspirations of the Epistle. The Semitic and the Christian elements are seen mingling with one another. They do that only by the instrumentality of the Epistle. In the end, the dual virtue of this testimony is to manifest, by means of a native document,

[1] That is *Cod. Bernensis* and *Cod. Wissenburgensis* (*Acta*, Nov. ii, i, 104).

[2] Reading of *Cod. Bern.* (*op. cit.* 34).

the Antiochian connexions of the Epistle to the Hebrews.[1]

" We have come unto Zion, mount and city of the living God ; and to myriads of angels in the assembly and church of the enrolled firstborn in the heavens, to the spirits of just men made perfect ; and to God the judge of all, to Jesus the mediator of the new covenant ; and to blood of sprinkling[2] which speaketh better things

---

[1] The only Passio septum fratrum Machabaeorum I have examined is in Cod. 9389, fol. 197–200 of the Imperial Private Library, Vienna. Through the courtesy of the Hofbibliothekar rotographs of the document were sent to me. Its date is the fifteenth century. The writing is in a Renaissance hand. It is defective, lacking one folio. In character a prolix document. Its two parts, the refusal to partake in porcine ritual and the martyrdom of the seven, are highly developed. The site of the martyrdom is not given. The whole document impresses one as probably having received its present form at Latin hands from a shorter Greek original. The ancient note in it to which attention may be drawn is the use of " confessores " for the Maccabees. Long before the fifteenth century they were recognised as martyrs. Also ecclesiastical language had then been long accustomed to make distinction between the two terms and their application. As far back as the Letter to Vienne and Lyons (Eusebius, Hist. Eccl. v, ii, 3), that distinction was made. We have seen already that the Syrian Martyrology called the Maccabees " confessors." That is what the Syriac word " modina " means. Severus of Antioch, as we have seen, filled out the term by adding the word for " martyrs." It seems then that in this late use of the term " confessores " we have the lingering influence of the original Syriac account of the Maccabees and its designation of them. In the light of the discoveries made concerning them and the Epistle to the Hebrews it is a likely suggestion that this designation arose from the verb ὁμολογήσαντες in Heb. xi, 13.

[2] This is probably a reflection from the Torah lection of Tammuz, Numbers xxviii f., with its sacrifices for the community. Cf. Exodus xxix, 20 f., where the practice of sprinkling, both altar and ground and man, is mentioned in the consecration of those who will offer those sacrifices. We must not forget the inwoven ideas of High-priest and community.

than that of Abel. Take heed that ye refuse not the Speaking One."[1]

Everything changes from terms of locality into categories of life. That is the major fact of the revelation. " We have not come " to cult sociology and topography : " we have come " to the God of Life and the society of men made alive in and through the Revealer. The seekers come alway to One who does and speaks, and never to cult or place. They ask " where have we come ? " The guide replies : " ye are come to Him who is Zion and temple and encompassing life to all who believe in Jesus Christ."

We must break away, for some moments, from the religious appreciation of the Epistle's close to study its structure. Thus light is thrown on the writer's art and thought. It is the constant duty of his interpreter to do this. It should be as frequent a duty for the appraiser of his thought ; thus he would be kept from giving it wings of foreign theory. This magnificent climax to the Epistle is an epitome of its structure and thought. The filaments of the web here manifest their pattern. It is all of golden truth. The contrast " we have not come " and " we have come " can be followed back, thread by thread, to source and each stage in the progress of thought : the fears of the exiled mind and the faith of the Christian mind. The subjects of Ab and Tammuz and the influence of Torah and prophetical lections display the design for which they were chosen. This will be seen most

[1] The over-many conjunctions are troublesome. It is clear that the sense of this passage must be ruled by the thought of the whole Epistle.

clearly through some of its details. " The church of
the enrolled firstborn in the heavens and the spirits of
just men made perfect," is a first illustration. The
words epitomise chapter xi. Their threads also run
back to the earlier ideas of Peace and Rightness. This
the verb " made perfect " brilliantly indicates. The
same bright quality is in the use of the plural of " firstborn." That concept and term is deeply inlaid in the
earlier idea of the Semitic community. It is as
profoundly integral to the greater concept of the
community of Jesus Christ : wherein each of its
members is as a firstborn to the Firstborn. There can
be no reference in these words from the Epistle to the
myth of Jesus' descent into the place of the dead.[1] That
may be an Antiochian growth of the second century.[2]
Our writer refers to the earthly phase of the immortal
community : the complement to that which is in the
heavens. This reference to the perfecting of spirits is
another way of describing the psychic community.
It fails to convey the writer's meaning if it is made to
refer to extra-terrestrial achievement. He does now
with silver-point brevity what he had done before on a
large canvas in chapter xi.

Again, the reference to Abel is not merely a glance
back to the same chapter. It is a re-emphasis of the
fact that he is present because he has community
values. No filiation of a doctrinal sort, and with
regard to the idea of sacrifice, is being made out

---

[1] *E.g.*, Loofs in Hastings *Encyclopædia of Religion and Ethics*,
iv, 662.

[2] *Cf. Odes of Solomon*, xlii. Moffatt, 218, appears to think that
Hebrews ii, 14, makes another reference to this descent ; but see
supra, c. ii.

between him and Jesus Christ. The context is
shadowlessly clear on that point. It has no sense of
typology ; but only that of community. The Semitic
concept is in service to its wonderful transmutation,
the " Body of Christ." A third illustration of the
intellectual basis of the climax is manifest in its use of
Haggai ii.[1] It is also an exquisite indication of the
writer's workmanship. This prophet is awake in his
memory because he is dealing with the subjects of the
great Fasts—the rebuilding of the Temple in his own
and Zechariah's time. The citation is linked by
natural necessity with the subject of Joshua which is
from the Lectionary and is in the Epistle. He is
pictured in Haggai, it should be noted, as a king-priest.
Thus our writer inweaves at the end of his work
another indication of his ancillary use of the Siwan
prophetical lection.[2] A last instance is in the words
" unto Zion, mount and city of the living God." The
Centre concept of the cosmos, which is Jerusalem, that
main essential of the Semitic community in all periods
of Israelitish thought, is also the main essential of the
climax to the Hebrews. It would have to be. Its
writer is doing as was done by the writer of the
Apocalypse ; he is transmuting the ancient civic and
cosmic Centre by the energies of the revelation of
Jesus Christ.[3] It is easy to see how the lesser and
greater prefaces fit this magnificent close to the Epistle,

[1] Hebrews xii, 26.
[2] See *supra,* c. iv.
[3] The adjective in the phrase " heavenly Jerusalem " is a
cosmic one rather than a religious one. The city must not be put
in the sky as if it were an eschatological city. On the name
Jerusalem with its community values, see Cook, 402.

if we are true to the Hebrew documents and ideas from which it was composed. Both are necessary for its understanding up to its last word and structural note.

It is time to resume the religious assessment of the Epistle. " We have not come . . . we have come " —the writer and the exiles have gone from Sinai to Zion. One is a peak on the cult map of Palestine, the other is the dominating height on the map of the human spirit. Both are landmarks in the history of religion. For Western religion they are the two poles. Though we shall be wise to remind ourselves again that before either of them had gained such a high estate, each was a mountain of the Centre of the cosmos and cult of the Western Semites.[1] We have to reconsider this trek from Sinai unto God. It begins on a mount in a desert : and it ends in the most fruitful and vital context for human personalities. We miss one half of the glory of the achievement, if we say that it began on the earth and ended in heaven. That makes it a topographical feat. So also is the adventure robbed of another essential significance, if we say that it is a going on from Moses to Jesus. That makes it an evolutionary feat. The loss is as disastrous, if we reduce the quest to a parable of the transit of man from this world to the next. Since that makes it an allegorical feat. The writer's " we have come " is not an anticipation of what Bunyan did. He is writing to exiles who, like himself, are on the earth ; and of an attained object. They

---

[1] See *Book of Jubilees*, viii, 19 ; Gressmann, *Der Ursprung der israelitisch—jüdischen Eschatologie* (1905), 183, on Sinai as the Centre.

start from Sinai, because it is a Centre in a cult : they reach Zion, because that Centre has been transmuted into the spiritual goal of the revelation of Jesus Christ. We have to remember always that the Epistle was first written to Semites.

The writer's two axial phrases, " we have not come . . . we have come," mark then no steady climb from the lowlands to the highlands, but an uprooting of man from the hold of the ways behind him that he might live in the true and immortal context for life and mind. This means a most rigorous and open-eyed achievement.

Those two phrases form, indeed, the axis of the Epistle. The Silent Voices and the lowland ways are in antithesis to the Revealer and His revelation. The structure of the Epistle turns on them. It has been said that it is composed with such delicacy, that the writer has reproduced the exile's mental conditions. The axial phrases with their tonic messages meet each haunting fear and vagrant step. The question which faces both behind and before : " which way will we go ? " is answered by the messenger of the revelation : " we have not come . . . we have come." It checks the man who would turn again to the ways of the ancient world : it enables him to reach at once his home in God. The answer is according to Christian metabiology, and not one in religious geography. The quest is always on to life or back to conditions which make against life. Therefore, we must realise that the writer's intent is to show to his readers that check and enabling are as alive, in their everyday experience, as the ebb and flow of their wills between the Past and God.

He is not trying to bring them to any formal end of things, which will be very different from the scenery among which they began. He is as little moved by the idea of an end of things as by the dramatic finality, which rules most of us, that death is of necessity a powerful wizard with scenery. His " we have come " can be spoken as a man steps from this hour to that, it is the moment he turns his head to look straight on, and this he may do even on any dusty road of the world ; or when he reaches some far-off post in the cosmos, perhaps beyond the veils of Sirius on a morning which no calendar now counts. Whenever and wherever men can turn or go on—the check or enabling of God is at work.

The writer of the Epistle thus has his own most lovely style of writing the term and the truth of the *Parousia:* the Presence of God. He is where men truly seek Him, and there in all the powers of the revelation of Jesus Christ. A man determines to listen to Him and no longer to the Silent Voices ; he stumbles along the new way, and after a short essay stops to ask : " where am I ? " The answer is : " thou hast come to God and Life and alive men." The same answer is given to the most saintly as he or she comes to that strange over-shadowing we call death. It will be the same everywhen and everywhere in the cosmos. For God is Life and Temple and Universe for men. He and all that is He is where human beings follow Jesus Christ.

We post-date Him ; and make Him as Temple and Enfolder of the society of His disciples in the drama of the Last Things. When we do that, we go back to the powers unto death for man of the cults of the ancient world. Another glance over this remarkable close to chapter xii will show that each of its phrases overthrows each of the objects which allured men back to the lowland ways. There is no more the reign of cosmic and cult site but God; no more Jerusalem but God in whom men live; no more angels of the Idea but men alive in God; no more menaces like those of Ab and Tammuz but God's will unto life for men; no more a covenant for the maintenance of a primitive Semitic society but Jesus the Revealer and the energies and truth of the covenant unto life for human beings : His community which is now and for ever. The message of the Epistle is for all the ages, since man will never overcome the lure of the lowland ways nor cast off the spell of the Silent Voices except by the revelation of the Lord Jesus Christ.

PRINTED IN GREAT BRITAIN BY MACKAYS LIMITED, CHATHAM